GRASPING SOCIAL MEDIA

The Social Media Journey of A Baby Boomer

MATT ENGLISH

ISBN: 149601488X
ISBN 13: 9781496014887
Library of Congress Control Number: 2014903623
CreateSpace Independent Publishing Platform
North Charleston, South Carolina

To my amazing wife, Anne, and our four children and partners, Douglas (and wife Mandy), Peter (and Georgie), Annabelle, and Caroline, who have been fearless friends, critics, and supporters on my journey

Table of Contents

INTRODUCTION

For travellers visiting Europe in years gone by, one of the great means of moving around was by train using a Eurail train pass. This pass entitled the user to unlimited travel by train and was a popular way of travel for baby boomers (just like me!) visiting Europe in the 1970s and 1980s, especially before the advent of heavily discounted airfares between European cities. This fixed price pass continues today and is generally bought in the traveller's home country prior to arrival in Europe.

The Eurail pass opened up many options and opportunities for seeing different countries and cities. Moreover, it provided the opportunity to experience a journey of exploration. Some journeys were a straight point-to-point experience, such as travelling direct from, say, Paris to Frankfurt. But the Eurail pass enabled travellers to truly explore and see places in a different sequence, or indeed to come back and visit a place multiple times. The Paris to Frankfurt trip could well meander via Strasbourg, Stuttgart, and Koblenz, and could also involve faster or slower regional trains along the way. This was very much about the journey. Yes, there was always a sense of destination, but the excitement was as much about the experience of the journey, the places visited, and the friends made along the way.

I look at my experience with social media through the lens of a journey that has taken many twists and turns along the way and also involved some backtracking. It has been far from a straight-line experience. It has embraced major social media tools such as Facebook, Twitter, and LinkedIn, as well as broader activities, including blogs and chat rooms.

But social media is not just about the use of some neat technology. It is about real social change. In fifty years' time, when writers are casting the spotlight on the period from, say, 2005 to 2014, I suspect they will highlight social media as one of the great social phenomena of the time. I expect they will draw attention to the social impact it made across the globe, across different languages, and across different social divides. This social change is about both the personal and business aspects of social media and how these are blending together in ways never thought possible just a few years ago.

Yet social media is still an evolving experience and is shaping and reshaping itself for both personal and business applications. It has some way to go to come of age, although many believe that it will never come of age in the traditional sense. Rather, it will reach further levels of sophistication and use.

In the mid-2000s, I was well aware of social media but did not really understand it. At the time, I must admit it seemed like a bit of huff and bluster. The younger generation seemed to be obsessed with their friends via Facebook, but friendship as I knew it hinged around personal contact and real conversation. These features seemed to be slipping out the door thanks to social media, and I found this somewhat discomforting. It seemed that very personal and direct means of contact and communications were under serious challenge, but with little to replace them other than a computer screen.

But one day someone said to me that we should be careful not to focus too much on the tools and instead look at the outcomes. Sometimes when we receive gratuitous advice, we can take it personally and feel some resentment. But on this occasion, something caused me to ponder the advice further and think about the real message. I thought long and hard about it and came to the realization that I had to lever open my mind to focus on what social media was doing and, more importantly, what it could do in the future. The tools were far less important compared to the underlying social change that was happening.

So I started to look at social media in a totally different light and saw a whole new universe in front of me. I embarked upon a journey of discovery, which I found difficult and somewhat confusing at the start, but which has now evolved into one that is fun and fulfilling. Now any digital device I have with me at the time—smartphone, tablet, or computer—is effectively my digital Eurail pass. This enables me to engage, to connect, and to experience a world beyond.

This is my social media story, but it is far from finished. One of the things I have learned about social media is that it is constantly changing in so many ways. Like the chameleon, the face and colour of social media does change. But that is where the comparison ends, as the speed of change of social media is profound. This is not a book about the tools of social media or how to use different tools. Whilst I do mention various tools, the focus is very much on what social media can do and how it can expand our personal and business horizons. It is about how we can all benefit from this enormous social change that is evolving before our eyes.

Let the journey begin.

1

Approaching The Social Media Journey

I travel not to go anywhere, but to go. I travel for travel's sake. The great affair is to move.
                    —Robert Louis Stevenson

Social Media in Context

Let's step back a little and make sure we have a common understanding of what social media is and what it is not. Social media in one sense has been around for longer than we think.

The underpinnings of social media go back a long way in history. Since the beginning of humanity, individuals have felt the need to reach out and connect with their fellow human beings. In early times, this was done exclusively on a face-to-face basis. People meeting in the village square or farmers meeting at the local market formed the basis for social connection and an exchange of information of sorts. Over time, letters and other forms of communications became available. Later still, the telephone revolutionized communications and social contact.

More recently, the advent of computerization, and especially mobile communications, has changed the way that social connection happens. I clearly remember my first use of a mobile phone realizing that I could be in contact from almost anywhere and indeed could be contacted almost anywhere. But this was largely one-to-one social contact. Then there was the teleconference that was mostly used in business, but it did have the ability to connect many different people in many locations.

Social media has dramatically lifted all this to another level and created an exciting new playing field. To me, this shift is a bit like the US space program in the 1960s. Initially the single astronaut going into earth orbit atop an Atlas rocket was awe-inspiring. But a whole new level was reached later that decade when three astronauts could be transported atop the Saturn rocket and actually go to the moon and back. The technology was amazing, but the outcome defined a new era.

Likewise, social media is enabled by some impressive technology. As the era of both computerization and the Internet came together, the potential power of social media became enormous. Like the confluence of two great rivers, the scope and strength of both together created a whole new dimension. Early in my social media journey, I felt that some of what I was seeing was a bit underwhelming. I really did not want to see photos of my friends online. I found some of the daily updates of their holidays a bit tortuous. But over time, I came to realize that social media is radically different in some fundamental ways and that I needed to adopt a different perspective.

Social Media is so Different

Social media is different because of three fundamental characteristics, the combination of which we have never seen before. It is *instant*, *global*, and *transparent*.

The first of these is the *instant* nature of social media. Immediacy is a defining factor with social media. A picture can be uploaded the moment it is taken, or a comment can be issued and circulated immediately. I remember trying to get my head around the amazing concept of the so-called light year—the distance that light travels in one year. Now the Internet minute, or what happens on the Internet every minute, is the mind-stretching concept. Intel[1] has made some estimates of what happens every minute on the Internet, which include:

- One hundred thousand new tweets
- Six million Facebook views
- More than two million search queries on Google

---

1 *What Happens in an Internet Minute, Intel, September 2013.*

These numbers in themselves are staggering, but the underlying message is the enormous change in the reach of communications due to the instant nature of social media.

The tragedy at the Boston Marathon in 2013 highlighted the instant nature of social media. Images and reports were not only uploaded rapidly by hundreds of people but were also used by the authorities to help track down the perpetrators.

Another aspect of social media that has captured people's imagination is its truly *global* reach. One can easily connect with colleagues and friends across the globe. Global conversations, discussions, and information sharing can now occur easily and frequently. We can track our friends and family who are travelling abroad and enjoy their photos and commentary on a frequent basis. The global reach of social media is a major by-product of the growth and pervasiveness of networked devices.

Intel estimates that the number of networked devices in the world today is equal to the global population (i.e., about seven billion), whereas in 2015 it will be twice the global population. This growth is also supported by geographic penetration of the Internet showing that global Internet users have grown from 360 million in 2000 to 2.4 billion in 2012, an increase of some 5.6 times.[2] This growth has been especially prevalent in Asia, Europe, and the Middle East. Social media has been an integral part of that expansion.

The third aspect of social media that is different is that it is largely *transparent*. Whilst there are various ways of controlling access and privacy, there is a significant degree of transparency in social media across the board. For instance, we know that recruiters use social media activity as one input to assessing a candidate's suitability for a job. There is potentially a problem if language and comments in social media are somewhat borderline in their sentiment. We have all experienced the e-mail "accident" where a comment or some information was copied to the wrong recipient. Sometimes this is a simple mistake that is easily rectified, but in other situations it can be highly embarrassing or indeed a possible legal issue. By its nature, social media mistakes of this type can magnify the scale of the problem dramatically and can also make the retraction more difficult. When information or comments go viral on social media, they are difficult to rein in.

---

2 *Internet Growth Stats, June 2012.*

Social Media Does Matter

Remember life as it was in smaller communities in earlier times? Think of the English village or the Australian country town. These smaller communities shared some unique characteristics. Everybody knew each other and looked after each other, and the notion of privacy was minimal. Their citizens were well connected, and the sense of community was strong and personal.

But as technology changed, so too did the village. Consider the impact of transport. As various forms of transport became available, the village became accessible to others, and it also gave the villagers the opportunity to move to new places either for work or to explore. Other technology changes such as the telephone broke down the boundaries even more.

Today in the Western world, the traditional village has become a mere shadow of its former self as the world has become so urbanized. We still use the term *village*, but more in the context of the so-called global village. Bill Gates once said, "The Internet is becoming the town square for the global village of tomorrow".

This concept of the global village has rapidly evolved. Take the idea of travellers being connected. Not so many years ago, travellers had to post written letters home to friends and relatives, and chatting by phone was expensive and therefore a rare occurrence. But today travellers can be connected instantly via phone or the Internet and can even have face-to-face contact using online video tools.

This global village has really come alive in the past five years or so through the various forms of social media that have exploded on the scene. Local geographic constraints no longer define how people connect or interact. Technology has changed the playing field and indeed the language. People now "Google" something or "Skype" someone or "tweet". Such verbs did not exist until recently.

Of course, the global village is vastly different from the traditional village in many ways, especially in structure, appearance, and behaviour. For instance, in the global village, we deal with strangers very differently. How many friends have we accepted on Facebook that we hardly know? How many followers do we have on Twitter whom we have never met and indeed will not meet in a lifetime? How many times do we buy items from complete strangers on the other side of the planet? The traditional village was a far more intimate affair and much more self-contained. In those times, a stranger arriving at the village was therefore viewed as an outsider and probably greeted with some suspicion.

But it is instructive to see the factors that are common and to appreciate some of the lessons for our global village today, especially as they relate to social media. These are known as the three "Cs". Whilst each is important in its own right, it is the combination of all three that is significant in social media today.

The Three Cs: Connection

The traditional village provided a strong and very personal connection for its members. Indeed, it was the essential ingredient for making the village work successfully and was highly transparent and current. Connection was frequent, although in varying levels of intensity depending on one's position and level of importance in the village.

But over time, the notion of connection changed dramatically. In the last century, for instance, connection was focused on having one's physical diary or address book up to date, and lists of names, addresses, and phone numbers might be found in various paper forms. These were used as the basis for keeping in touch via a phone call or a letter, or indeed face-to-face visits.

Today the global village also provides connection, but across cities and the boundaries of nation-states, and at any time of day or night. Social media in particular has given huge impetus to this phenomenon. If we add up the users of Facebook, Twitter, and LinkedIn combined, it totals around a staggering two billion. Yes, there will be some overlap in the numbers, but the point is that these three social media platforms alone provide connection for an extraordinary percentage of the global population.

The interesting thing about the modern-day connection via social media is that whilst it takes place over the Internet and may seem impersonal, the connection can and does occur more frequently than ever. In my youth, a traveller might have sent a letter home a few times a month, whereas now there can be multiple contacts each day together with photos and commentary to add some colour to the content. In addition, these contacts today are two-way real-time experiences.

Another aspect of social media connection is its dynamic nature, especially in relation to second- and third-level connections. I may have a direct contact with you, but in the past your contacts would have been inaccessible to me. But with social media, it is easy to see your contacts and to gain connection with them—if they wish, of course. A whole new dynamic is emerging, with second- and third-level connection being used to expand contact and links between people across geography.

LinkedIn provides a strong example in the business context where people can connect with former colleagues by way of second-level contacts. That is, if you have lost contact with a former colleague, you may be able to reconnect with him or her via another person who still has contact with your former colleague. Moreover, this can be done very simply with the click of a button. The magnitude of the connections is massive. If you have, say, one thousand direct connections on LinkedIn, it could mean that you have millions of connections in your second- and third-level networks.

Of course, what you do with those connections is another matter, but the point is that social media provides a major step up in terms of the number of connections available and the speed and ease of making those connections. Business executives used to keep small boxes of business cards that made up the core of their network. They would be organized in either alphabetical order or sometimes in company order. Later, when computers emerged, the use of spreadsheets for managing connections became more widely embraced.

But all of this was very limiting from a number of aspects. In particular, the sharing of these contacts was very much one-dimensional or built around a hub-and-spoke model. That is, you were at the centre, or the hub, and all your contacts were at the end of the spokes. Now with social media, you can see how the spokes are connected and who is connected to whom, which takes the breadth and depth of connections to a whole new level.

This provides a major opportunity in the business context, but let's not forget the opportunities for greater personal contact and connection. Facebook has tapped this area with enormous success, and the ability to broaden one's group of contacts has been one of the major features of the social media revolution in the past five years or so.

The Three Cs: Community

The traditional village was about a real sense of community. People were involved and visible in the activities of the village, and they had to be part of the community making a contribution to its activity and to its ultimate success. Failure to do so would create a very difficult situation indeed. The strength of the community was fundamental to the growth and prosperity of the village. People were involved in activities where trust was inherent in what was done and where knowledge was shared amongst the community and handed down through the generations.

The modern global village is also about community. It is about bringing people together around common interests. LinkedIn, for instance, has over 1.5 million discussion groups covering a vast array of topics and items of interest. This is a very different form and scale from the traditional concept of community, but the fundamental thread of linking people via common interests is the same. The global village is about the sharing of information and experiences, but with the advantage of being able to link people across different parts of the world.

Communities on social media not only provide a basis for sharing of knowledge and information of common interest, but there is also the opportunity to quickly reshape communities as needed. Communities can be dismantled and reshaped and can change emphasis based on the needs of the community. This is a very fluid model and one that is dynamic in nature.

Online communities have exploded in the number and variety of topics. Whether it is a hobby or a sport or business interest, there will be some online community available to share information, news, or photographs. Take aviation as an example. The website www.airliners.net provides aviation enthusiasts with a forum for photographs and aviation news and information, as well as a chat room and other ways of connecting with fellow enthusiasts around the world. It claims to have eighty million page views per month from nine hundred thousand unique visits. It also cites over 1.2 million photographs for its community members and is increasing at over five hundred per day. This community can also link to the site via Facebook, meaning that regular information and photos are posted to the news feed on Facebook. This type of community is focused very strongly on the provision of information and the sharing of content. It is just one example of the myriad communities that are being formed or reformed on a daily basis.

Social media has also provided a broader opportunity for problem solving. For example, consider a user community for a product like the Apple iPad. Such a community exists to respond to queries on the use of the iPad or to share information on how to maximize the use of its functions. At any one time there could be over three hundred thousand discussions underway covering a range of topics from getting started to better use of e-mail or other functions. Remember, this is just one community for this one product, and these communities are mostly open and free.

Other communities exist for social or a broader set of discussions or contact. For example, there are thousands of communities for alumni groups from business school classes or former colleagues of organizations. These sites will typically have some vetting process in place to ensure that only legitimate members are included.

The notion of community via social media is endless in terms of the breadth and depth of what is available. It is vastly greater than what could have been imagined in earlier times.

The Three Cs: Collaboration

The notion of pulling together to get the job done was a strong feature of the traditional village. This collaboration provided the real glue that enabled the village to thrive. It involved collaborating on issues such as planting of crops or the defence and well-being of the village. Sure, there was a hierarchy to organize much of this, but at the end of the day the collaboration of the entire village was integral to its day-to-day success and prosperity.

Today the world of social media provides an extensive platform for collaborating around solutions to problems or gathering teams together for business activities such as product development. Retailers, for example, are using social media more and more for input to product development. I witnessed a retailer not so long ago put an interesting question on its Facebook page—how would you design the ideal shopping aisle? This question prompted many good suggestions from customers. This may not substitute for focus groups and more detailed research, but it did provide another channel of information that was immediate, relevant, and, most important, free to the retailer.

But there is another dimension here that social media brings to the table—its global reach. In the retail example above, input to the question came not only from existing customers in the local geography; others who were shopping at competitors or located overseas could also contribute. In other words, social media enabled the retailer to capture an array of ideas from around the world and therefore the widest possible set of experiences and ideas. This is where social media can be so powerful, because it can harness the breadth and depth of knowledge available from the global village. Used properly, social media can provide organizations and individuals with a wider lens for collaboration on problems or issues at hand.

Effective collaboration using social media is anchored around two features, namely the ability to post information quickly and easily and the visibility of that information. In the retail example above, the information was easy to enter on Facebook and was of course visible to all those who were participating. This gave participants an opportunity to not only see what others were saying but also the means to build on those ideas and reshape and mould their thinking as well. The outcome of the collaboration effort was much richer because of the number of ideas and how those ideas were refined and shaped along the way. The collaboration effort became a story of how an idea was developed, not just a static "suggestion box" of thoughts.

Direct involvement of customers is becoming a major avenue for organizations in many areas, including product development, service level assessment, and feedback of experience. The US airline JetBlue used Twitter extensively to communicate directly to its passengers in the event of flight changes or updates. If a flight was delayed due to, say, a late inbound aircraft, the airline could update passengers immediately and directly rather than relying solely on the airport departures board or announcements on the public address system.

Organizations can also use social media to collaborate internally on special projects or initiatives. In 2003, IBM did this on a global scale when it reshaped its corporate values. It called the process a "Values Jam" and involved the active online participation of tens of thousands of employees globally providing suggestions and comments on the values of the business. All this input needed to be assessed and distilled over time, but after several months the corporation announced its three corporate values. These values were of special significance because they had been developed with extensive input and collaboration from employees across the world. This is an excellent example of collaboration in action showing the power of how ideas can be harnessed in real time and refined into solid and enduring outcomes. Those values are still in place today and form a key feature of the way IBM operates.

Social media is a key element of the global village as we know it and will continue to grow in influence in this space. Technology has changed the village in shape and scale forever, but some of the underlying fundamentals are as important today as they were when the local village was the way of life.

"But Why Should I Bother?"

In my travels, I find that this question or a version of it comes up frequently. Despite the very impressive array of statistics showing the growth of social media, I still find plenty of people and businesses that pose this question and have a passive and sometimes quite hostile position against social media. Some of this is related to demographics, but there is a wider span across many age groups and businesses that sit in the nonbeliever camp.

They very quickly cite the things that have gone wrong with social media and some of the challenges that do occur from time to time. An inappropriate comment or photo that goes viral on social media will often attract negative publicity, which tends to cloud the broader social media debate. Inappropriate activity on social media needs to be pounced on and offenders need to be dealt with appropriately. But a small number of problems should not be the determining factor in deciding whether social media is good or bad. Traffic accidents are a blight on developed societies, but we still build roads and bring in rules and other factors to mitigate the problems. Likewise, governments and organizations are taking steps to ensure that the right standards of behaviour and conduct are managed on social media.

People or businesses may choose not to be involved in social media for any number of reasons. The decisions on the use of social media depend on many factors, such as peer pressure, previous experience in this area, or uncertainty about the social media space generally. They are also influenced by experiences they hear about directly or indirectly. People who are reluctant to embrace social media often have a quick and ready recall of things that may have gone wrong, such as comments or photos going viral and having unintended consequences.

On the positive side, think of social media as a broader communication and content channel, both for business and personal application. Yes, it is different from other channels in so many ways, but the mistake is often made to ignore what social media can achieve rather than the tools to do it. For instance, a small business wanting to expand its offerings to an established customer base can use social media to drive a broader conversation and indeed start new ones. Powerful conversations and interaction can be unleashed via social media, and in real time. But the business needs to have a clear view of what it is trying to achieve with social media. Whether the business chooses Twitter or Facebook or another tool is important, but this is secondary to the question of what it is trying to achieve.

From a personal perspective, social media opens up new horizons in so many ways. It provides individuals with windows into knowledge and information like never before. People also need to have a view of what really interests them. Are they seeking to engage with family and friends or simply find items of interest? The available content on social media from magazines and organizations is enormous and growing all the time. It used to be that the only way to gain access to articles from good magazines was to subscribe to them or use the local library to look at back copies. But now much of this is readily available via social media. Information feeds on Twitter and Facebook are pushing this material to a global audience, and everyone can participate.

Social Media is a Real Game Changer

Social media has grown at an explosive rate over the past five years, and the statistics are staggering. Consider the following data from Steven White, professor of marketing and international studies at Charlton College of Business, which highlights the CAGR (compound annual growth rate) of various social media from 2006 to 2012[3]:

- Facebook, 109%
- Twitter, 507%
- LinkedIn, 71%
- Word Press, 120%

Remember, this data is compound annual growth data and not just one or two years. It is hard to see this growth slowing in the foreseeable future, especially as more and more countries expand their social media footprint and as the age groups engaged in social media continue to broaden. Social media is also rapidly expanding in the world of business.

Social media provides a means of connection that is truly game changing, whether in a business or personal context. Communicating with a utility or a phone company or a retailer used to be a somewhat lengthy process. But now social media provides a quick and ready means of two-way communication. For instance, a bank recently had an outage in one of its Internet banking systems with the result that customers were not able to pay their bills online. On its Facebook page, the bank managed to keep customers informed not only by way of updates on the status of the problem but also by way of a real-time dialogue with customers. The ability to maintain connection with a wide range of customers in this manner provided a key communications channel for the bank and positive connection with the bank's customers. Whilst customers were not exactly applauding the

---

3 *Social Media Growth, 2006–2012, D. Steven White, PhD, Charlton College of Business, University of Massachusetts, 2013.*

system outage itself, the communications and openness of the Facebook dialogue was an important part of customer engagement and experience.

Individuals and organizations benefit strongly from the power of being connected. The tyranny of distance has rapidly eroded as social media enables contact for both personal and business purposes. Much of the focus of social media in its earlier days was heavily geared to personal contact. But in recent years, the use of social media by business and governments alike has risen dramatically. But in some respects we have only just begun. For all of us, the journey is now unfolding rapidly and setting us challenges and opening up opportunities. The power of social media is here indeed.

Key questions to consider

- *How would you describe your social media experience to date?*
- *How has social media helped you or your business to enhance connection, community, and collaboration?*
- *Do you see social media as a feature of convenience or a vital tool for the future and why?*

2

The Journey Unfolds

You know more of a road by having travelled it than by all the conjectures and descriptions in the world.
                                        —William Hazlitt

Social Change is Taking Hold

Over the centuries, some extraordinary landmarks of enduring achievement have punctuated the journey of humanity. Think of the ancient Greeks and their achievements regarding learning and philosophy. The Romans stand out because of their organization and empire-building skills as well as infrastructure. The oceanic explorers such as Columbus, Magellan, and Cook expanded the world far beyond the imagination and perspectives at the time. These and other major achievements not only defined an era but also heralded a step change for humanity at that time.

Fast forward fifty or more years from now, and it will be interesting to see how writers describe our place in the sun, especially the 1990s and the 2000s. What will they say and how will they view our achievements? I suspect the Internet and the digital world will rank very high and will be seen as truly transforming our society in so many ways and with truly global impact. Whether this is viewed with the same aura as the Romans or the Greeks remains to be seen.

But I also suspect that future writers will give social media a special highlight for the era in which we live, both in terms of its impact on individual behaviour and society overall. Social media is frequently lauded for the way it has changed human interaction. Social information and photos on Facebook are often cited as significant and beneficial additions to how we connect with each other. On Twitter, expanded business opportunities through better direct engagement with customers are widely seen as transforming the way organizations do business.

However, focusing on the tools in social media misses the broader point: that social media is about a journey of social change, and we are only now starting to grasp its potential implications. As outlined in the previous chapter, social media brings entirely new levels of connection, community, and collaboration and is changing the way that people relate to each other. Individuals are connecting to each other differently, but they are also connecting differently with businesses, government agencies, and organizations. Connection, community, and collaboration occur all at the same time via social media, and this is being formed and re-formed as needs change. Social media not only provides the glue to make this happen but also serves as the accelerator that enables it to occur with great speed.

This speed of change is possibly the most exciting but also daunting aspect of the social media era. What happens in the Internet minute referenced in chapter 1 highlights the degree to which life has changed even in the past five years. How all this will play out and how social change will unfold into the future is hard to answer at this time. But the overall nature of social media provides a new way of sharing information, exchanging views, being involved in community thinking and activities, and harnessing new and interesting ideas. This social change is affecting both individuals and organizations alike. It is affecting all aspects of our lives even if we do not fully appreciate it at the time. Areas like national security, weather forecasting, service levels in retailing, health-care policies, political processes, and education are all affected in some way by social media.

One of the underpinnings of this social change is that information flow, and therefore decision making, is changing dramatically. Gone are the days of information being controlled and managed via corporations or organizations making or selling goods and services. As the saying goes, information is power, and that power is rapidly shifting.

First Steps and Some Sense of Direction

So how do we make the most of such social change and where do we begin? Like any new endeavour in life, the first steps into social media can take many forms. One thing I have learned over the years is there is no uniform way of starting the journey into social media. There is no "one size fits all" model. Some people just begin through a combination of peer pressure and some inherent interest in the subject. Others wait longer to take the plunge and possibly ease themselves into it over a long period of time.

When you learn the principles of, say, accounting, there is almost a set sequence of learning, such as understanding the notion of debits and credits and the concept of the balance sheet. When a pilot learns to fly, there are defined issues and procedures to learn, many of which can be practised in a simulator. But it is not so with social media, which presents an array of choices of what can be used and how to use it. Notwithstanding the massive growth in social media, over the years many individuals and smaller businesses have found it a bit confusing and perhaps too hard, and many have become the armchair commentators on the subject. They may have plenty of thoughts, but not a lot of direct experience.

A useful starting point is to understand that social media has redefined the way information and knowledge are shared and how business is done. In days gone by if we wanted information about a topic, we would seek it out from a library or an organized database of information that was held in some central location. In essence, we would use a "pull" type of system to bring that information to us, and this concept has provided the foundation of knowledge management over the past several generations.

But social media takes us in the other direction as it provides a very strong "push" model that complements the traditional "pull" approach. Thanks to technology, the "push" approach is revolutionary because it is instant, global, and transparent. Facebook, with over one billion registered users worldwide (and growing), enables the push of a huge variety of information to many different individuals, groups, and geographies. Twitter generates some five hundred million tweets every day, many of which push valuable information to recipients across the globe.

It is this "push" of social media that effectively creates the flood of information in all its forms. However, the push of social media is not a one-size-fits-all proposition. It helps to think about this point in three broad categories as follows:

- The social push
- The business push
- The information and knowledge push

The Social Push

This category has social interaction as its main objective and includes such things as the push of photos or the details of holidays to friends, family, and connections. Many people have experienced the photo side of social media from Facebook or more recently from Instagram. This aspect of social media is popular and generally a lot of fun. People can quickly share their experiences with friends and colleagues, and this is often the case for holiday photos. Remember the time when you had to wait to arrive home to share your holiday photos? Well those days are long gone, as social media has provided the mechanism to show your holiday photos in real time, and with two-way dialogue as well. This is a standout feature of social media, and for many people it is often the first thing that comes to mind when asked about the meaning of social media.

A few years ago at a conference, I chaired one of the breakout sessions with about fifty people in the room. I asked for a show of hands about what immediately came to mind when I mentioned the term social media. To help the discussion, I offered three choices: social chat, information, or commerce. Well over half the hands went up for social chat. This was a simple straw poll of one audience, but the story is often repeated, and generally the social push is seen as very prominent.

The social push embraces the sharing of experiences amongst friends in ways that were impossible a few years ago. Think of a dinner at a restaurant, for example. Through social media, we can now circulate comments on our experiences quickly to a wide audience, providing feedback that can be good or bad. Sites like TripAdvisor actively seek comments and feedback about hotels, restaurants, and tourism destinations.

Comments on social media about a good or bad experience can gain traction or go viral very rapidly. This is why many organizations that deal directly with consumers have people in their business constantly monitoring social media so they can quickly intercept and respond to any negative issues emerging on social media. This is a massive shift in how the world works, and interestingly, it is fusing together the individual and business implications of social media.

The social push also includes messages from celebrities to their social media fans stating, for example, that they have just landed in New York and the weather is cold. I am not sure this is adding significantly to the world bank of knowledge, but the fans probably think it is important. The popularity of this truly social dimension has been enormous and has without doubt been a major underpinning for social media platforms such as Facebook.

The Business Push

Sales, product development, product information, and product conversations are the main areas of activity here. Organizations have made great strides in recent years to really tap into the business opportunities that social media provides. Whilst this is still an evolving space for many organizations, there is already a huge uplift in the number of organizations actively engaged in social media with specific business objectives in mind. A recent report from the University of Massachusetts, Dartmouth,[4] shows the growing adoption of social media by the Fortune 500. For instance, in 2013, 77 percent of the Fortune 500 had Twitter accounts with a tweet in the previous thirty days. Social media is on the map for big business.

But here is the catch for business. This is not just about a series of comments and conversations in cyberspace for the general interest of readers. On the contrary, social media has major implications for the way consumers consider their purchasing decisions and therefore has serious impact for business. Consumers are strongly influenced by what their friends and colleagues are saying on social media and are making buying decisions accordingly. This direct consumer influence has profound implications for business.

This influence has always existed in some form or another. For example, consumers have been involved in focus groups or product discussion forums for a long time. But technology has changed this dramatically, and today consumers have instant access to global communications and connectivity via a raft of online sources such as social media, chat rooms, blogs, and so on. This has enabled a major change by placing enormous power in the consumers' hands, thus creating a new wave of direct consumer influence.

To illustrate, IBM[5] conducted some important research into consumer buying behaviour across some thirty thousand consumers globally. It found

---

4 *Social Media Adoption in the F500, University of Massachusetts, Dartmouth, 2013.*
5 *Capitalizing on the Smarter Consumer, IBM, 2011.*

that about 70 percent trusted friends, relatives, and customer reviews for their purchasing decisions compared to just 13 percent who relied on the retailers and suppliers. Much of that information from friends comes via the Internet, especially social media.

In parallel with this, a further major factor for social media in business today is the continuing growth and change in consumerism occurring globally and across all industry groups. The term "consumerism" only gathered common use back in the 1960s and '70s. Consumerism today has come about through the convergence of three factors:

- The expanding choice of products and services offered to consumers
- The growth of channels to supply those products and services
- The expanding purchasing power of consumers and the increase in individual wealth over the past fifty years

For business, this raises the challenge of the snowballing effect of consumer sentiment and commentary. A report from the Boston Consulting Group[6] highlights this and underscores the notion of advocacy marketing. This is where consumers not only support a product by buying it but also become its advocates on social media through favourable reviews, recommendations, or comments. Social media therefore can become a key strategic tool for business.

There are other aspects for business to consider in respect of social media. One relates to offerings and sales where businesses can make a direct sales pitch via social media and use this medium to not only generate interest but also to make sales. Organizations in travel and leisure are strong players in this arena, and offers of hotel accommodation and airfares are very frequently posted on social media. Businesses that act as consolidators of these offers are becoming very popular, in some ways akin to local travel agents about thirty or so years ago.

The Information and Knowledge Push

The explosion of data is accelerating. It is often said that most of the world's existing data was created in the past few years. *Science Daily*[7] maintains that 90 percent of the world's data has been created in the past two years

---

6 *Harnessing the Power of Advocacy Marketing*, Boston Consulting Group, 2012.

7 *Science Daily*, May 2013.

alone. The point is that the amount of data and information is expanding dramatically, which in turn allows us to access and harness so much more information and knowledge than was ever thought possible.

Thirty minutes on social media and Internet search engines today can generate an array of relevant and useful information that was impossible even a few years ago. Information releases that are pushed on social media have become not only prevalent but also extremely popular with users. Leading magazines and journals are now circulating massive amounts of quality information that is readily digestible by readers.

This has been helped along by user-friendly consolidation and filtering tools, such as Flipboard for the iPad. Flipboard is free and provides the user with access to key news and items of interest from a diverse range of organizations and publications. It sorts and organizes information for each of the publications and presents it in summary form. The user can then select items of interest for more detailed reading with the option to further share it with friends and colleagues or the wider community via social media. For instance, you may read a particularly interesting piece from a publication and then choose to share it via, say, LinkedIn or Facebook or both. In that way, the information and knowledge push gains even greater momentum.

Twitter, for instance, provides an effective means of distributing key items of information from many different sources. Following the *New York Times* or the BBC on Twitter will provide key news or features in a short and easy to read format. Many media outlets provide such a facility. In addition, major business publications such as the *Harvard Business Review* also post major articles and items of interest. Many of these are in blog formats that are easy to read and also provide some discussion forums. In other words, it is not just about receiving the information but the ability to participate in a dialogue as well.

The list of publications and organizations providing such access is endless. I particularly enjoy the ones that offer feature articles and commentary such as *The Economist* or the *World Economic Forum*. Others will have strong interest in hobbies or maybe science, both of which have extensive material in circulation on social media.

Concept of "User Pull"

Of course, the three areas above can all revert to a pull model whereby a user can interrogate social media tools to proactively seek and obtain specific pieces of information. In other words, the user can "pull" the information or content. For instance, a user can subscribe to an e-mail notification to obtain regular updates on content from various sources, or in other cases, such as a "like" on Facebook, the user can receive updates on his or her personal timeline. It is said that more than one million websites are now automatically linked to Facebook, which facilitates the idea of user pull.

As another example, Twitter provides information that is partly "push", but also very much "user pull". In the first instance, Twitter provides an interesting push model by way of very short statements that are 140 characters maximum. Any post on Twitter is limited to this simple formula, and if you exceed the limit of 140 characters, the excess characters simply do not get posted. This is a very clear and simple push approach and has created a whole new culture of abbreviated stories and headlines.

On the other side of the equation, the pull aspect is very strong. For example, a user may be "following" *The Economist* magazine. A post from this magazine may contain a very short Twitter statement, but it could be coupled with a link to an article or a blog that expands and illustrates the short statement. In this instance, the reader may be attracted by the short statement and may then be inclined to open the link and "pull" in the detail of the story or article. This is very much in the realm of "user pull".

In future years, how will the balance of this push and pull evolve, and how will the dynamics be played out? For example, how will the blending of the three areas above play out in the future and what will be the emphasis? I suspect there may be no definitive answer other than it will be changing constantly. However, what is clear from the explosive growth of social media is that people are not just talking about it but are getting rapidly engaged in all its forms, both as individuals and as businesses and governments.

Indeed, future writers may well say that we have taken to heart the lyrics of an Elvis Presley song: "A little less conversation, a little more action please".

Different Ways to Use Social Media

How people use social media is the topic of frequent conversation. Some will say they just "love Facebook" or they are spending a "lot of time on Pinterest" and so on. But there is a broader perspective here beyond just the social media sites these people use, and I have found it helpful to consider user behaviour in social media along two dimensions.

One is the frequency of use of social media, recognizing that some people are casual or infrequent users and may view social media to be somewhat incidental to their personal or business lives. At the other end of this scale, some people are very heavily involved in the use of social media and may well be obsessed with it. For these people, it may be that they access social media in some form every hour of every day.

The other dimension relates to the type of use of social media. Some people may focus only on the personal side, such as connections and contacts with friends, the sharing of photos of their travels, and so on. Typically this is more conversational, and the main objective is the contact rather than the content. Others will be more content focused and use social media to access a wide range of information and knowledge on their topics of interest, whether news and current affairs, history, or hobbies. Communities of interest on social media form an important part of information and content sharing.

Figure 1 below blends these two dimensions and highlights four major categories of how people use social media.

Figure 1 - Social Media User Behaviour

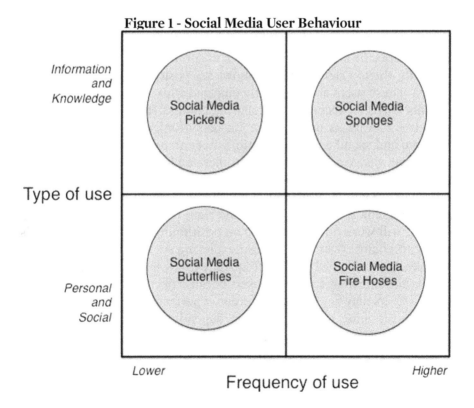

The first of these in the bottom left quadrant is the group labelled Social Media Butterflies. Their behaviour is focused on personal and social use, such as contact and conversations with friends, but with somewhat infrequent use. These users may access their social media sites on a very infrequent basis or may be quite passive in the way they participate. In other words, they may have a burst of activity when they have some spare time or when they go on holidays, for example.

The Social Media Fire Hoses shown in the bottom right quadrant of the matrix are also aligned to personal and social activity, but are high-frequency users. Their activity on social media is not only highly visible but also very intense in terms of frequency and profile. They are heavy users of social media that forms a significant part of their daily lives. They will be active through their smartphones and tablets, ensuring they can and do participate whenever and wherever they are. Frequent personal and social connection is vital to this group.

The top left quadrant of the matrix shows the so-called Social Media Pickers who are not frequent users of social media but will access particular information and knowledge when they require it. Their focus is more on content rather than contact. For instance, they may access the social media sites for certain magazines or journals, or they may explore information on specific areas of interest such as sport.

Finally, the top right quadrant shows the position of the Social Media Sponges. These users are frequently engaged with social media, but with the major focus on accessing and sharing content. They may have linked themselves to various media sites, journals, thinks tanks, consultancies, and so on, and spend considerable time on content by accessing information and knowledge across a range of topics and interests.

One of the great features and exciting aspects of social media is its multitude of potential uses and how different people will approach the way social media is used. But there is no right or wrong positioning here. Everyone will work out his or her own positioning and balance, and this is likely to change over time. Those exploring social media for the first time may start tentatively as low-frequency users, but over time they may find they become high-frequency users because of contact with family and friends. Others may have a very different experience.

The positioning may also change depending on particular circumstances. For instance, when people are travelling, their friends could be in the category of Social Media Butterflies and be well engaged with those travellers, but then change to another pattern of use when the travel is completed. On the other hand, when those friends are planning their own trips they may well be Social Media Pickers as they scour sites for information and commentary on various places to see and stay.

The pattern may also vary depending on the tools being used. A person may be a Social Media Butterfly on Facebook and access photos or family contacts from time to time, but at the same time may be a Social Media Sponge on Twitter and follow many business and media sites that provide regular updates on articles of interests.

The above discussion focuses on individual use, but the same broad principles are important in organizations and how they engage in their social media journey. Organizations will need to think carefully about what they want from social media, and hence the type and frequency of social media use will become key elements of how that strategy is executed. There is a more comprehensive discussion of the business issues around social media in chapter 4.

Some Encouragement

Many people I meet have a natural aversion to social media or at least a very strong degree of scepticism. Surprisingly, this is not restricted to the so-called older generations. Despite all the statistics, the Gen Xers and Gen Yers have their fair share of reluctant starters when it comes to social media. I am reminded of a conversion involving a Gen X man who was boasting about all the technology he owned. He proclaimed the virtues of his PC, his tablet, and his smartphone, and how they were all linked and backed up. This was overshadowed by the size and variety of his music collection, and it all sounded very impressive. But I was staggered by the admission that he totally shunned the use of social media. In fact, he made the extraordinary statement that he would never go near social media, and he exhorted others in the conversation to do likewise. It was akin to a mountaineer approaching a mountain with all the right equipment to do the job, but simply turning away at the base and going in another direction.

Is an act of faith needed to get into social media? Yes is the short answer, but it does not have to be a daunting or risky experience. I have found there are four principles that provide encouragement to anyone on the journey:

- *Try it.*
- *Understand it.*
- *Go for it.*
- *Select it.*

The first and simplest piece of advice is to *try it*, even if it is just putting a toe in the water. Use family members or friends to introduce you to social media, whether it is a foray into Facebook or Twitter. This is not just looking over someone's shoulder and viewing a sample screen. It truly needs to be your own registration on a social media site as this is your experience to own. Initially it may be very tentative, and there is nothing wrong with that. When I first joined Facebook, I caused some amusement amongst family members by only using the "like" button. It took me some time to work up the required courage to make my own post and share some content.

The second principle is to *understand* how the social media site operates. What are its dynamics, who is contributing, is it interesting and helpful? Initially social media sites can seem daunting, and you may need some time to really understand how to get the most out of them. Many sites now have good guidelines on how they can be used well and also various chat rooms that provide some really helpful tips and tricks. It is also important to persevere at this point and not be overwhelmed by some of the functions of social media that may seem foreign or difficult to follow.

Another principle is to develop a strong level of participation—to *go for it*. I learned very early on that in one sense you get out of social media what you put into it. Put another way, a passive participant will not harvest the full rewards of social media. People who join a social media site and sit back passively to wait for things to happen will be frustrated very quickly. I have heard people say they gained nothing from, say, Facebook even though they had been on Facebook for a few years. When it is revealed that these people contributed virtually nothing online and hardly participated in the Facebook community, it is not surprising that they found the experience somewhat underwhelming. Participation does not have to be extensive from day one. Indeed, in my experience, one needs to build to a level of participation and involvement that is appropriate to individual circumstances.

But the key point is that participation is the important factor here. Social media will not just come to you and give you an exciting experience. You have to reach out, which is not that difficult as there are many people in exactly the same position. It is important to check regularly on the social media sites of your choice as things are happening on social media every minute of every day. You may also want to circulate an article or a comment or just provide a "like" to something that attracts your fancy. Over time, as you participate more and more, you will find that some momentum starts to build and that a social media routine starts to happen. It may be, for example, that you spend time on social media for, say, thirty minutes every morning over coffee, and this becomes built into the natural routine. This practice can continue whether you are on holidays or travelling given the mobile devices and applications now available.

The fourth and final principle is about being *selective*. Over time, people will find the aspects of social media that suit them and other aspects that are not relevant to their needs. Some will find that using social media for day-to-day information is more suited to them, whereas others will find that the social and contact features are what work for them. Again, there is no right or wrong answer here, and everyone will find a level and a way of using social media that suits them. Being selective also provides the opportunity to gain a deeper benefit from social media. For example, a strong focus on gaining information via Twitter can prove very rewarding as various sites are explored and developed over time.

In discussions about social media, I often find there is too much focus on the tools and how they should be used. Make no mistake about it, the tools and different forms of social media are very important in the way that social media is used and how it delivers value. But the focus of this chapter has been about some higher-level issues, especially around what social media can do, how it helps people connect, and how it enables them to do different things. It is very much about the underlying social change that is occurring and driving changes in behaviour between individuals and between individuals and organizations. It is this social change that makes the social media journey both exciting and somewhat daunting.

Key questions to consider

- *How would you describe your experience in the social media "push" (social, business, or information and knowledge) and what benefits have you derived from these?*
- *Where are you placed on the Social Media User Behaviour Matrix and how has that changed over time?*
- *Considering the four principles (try it, understand it, go for it, select it), where are you positioned and what are your proposed next steps?*

3

Enjoying the Journey

I never did a day's work in my life. It was all fun.
—Thomas Edison

The Enjoyment Factor

Franklin D Roosevelt was credited with saying, "It is fun to be in the same decade with you". That sentiment can be extended to the fun we have with family or friends or colleagues. Often, our fondest memories of journeys are the ones captured in an old photo album or a file of contemporary digital photos. Sometimes a magnificent scene such as a special sunset may capture our attention, but mostly the photos of people having fun are the ones that stand out.

The fun factor in social media is not to be underestimated, and one of the great features of social media is the enjoyment of participation. Many find it almost an elixir that cures the more tedious effects of the day-to-day routine of life. In years gone by, the definition of fun was a localized one, and the local park or picture theatre may well have been the extent of it. But enjoyment from the Internet has taken us to a new level, and fun, especially from social media, is now built into daily activity.

Every journey has its moments of sheer excitement, whether it is rounding the corner to see a sight for the first time or meeting a former colleague who has been out of our lives for many years. The human mind is powerful regarding associations with events or places and embedding those images or feelings in its memories forever. How many times do we hear a song play on the car radio and remember exactly where we were when we first heard it maybe ten or twenty years earlier? I clearly remember stepping out of the train at Zermatt in Switzerland for the first time and seeing the mighty Matterhorn framed against a clear blue sky. It was one of those moments of special excitement that has stayed with me since.

The world of social media is no different as it also provides moments of excitement that will last and last. Connecting with friends or acquaintances via social media may seem impersonal and indifferent to many people, and in one sense that is true. Yet in another way, that connection may not have happened if social media was not there. In other words, social media can and does play a key part in enabling connections that might not otherwise occur. For me the exciting moments fall into four buckets.

1. Lost and Found

The first of these is making connections that have been lost for some reason. A work colleague from many years ago moved from Australia to the United States, and as a result we lost track of each other over time. But one day I spotted the person's name on social media, and within a short time we were reconnected and will catch up again in person when we are in the same place. This is but one example of how social media can help people connect and reconnect around the world. In fact, this is happening hour by hour at a staggering rate, whether the connections are personal or based on work and professional activities. This ability to connect and reconnect is a fun part of social media and of course can be done so easily.

LinkedIn is a prominent site intended more for business and professional connections. It is said there are some eleven thousand professional searches conducted every minute on LinkedIn. It provides a number of features, including updates on job changes or promotions. For instance, if one of my connections is promoted to a new role, a note to this effect will appear on my LinkedIn home page, and I have the option to send this person a note or comment of congratulations. This of course relies on the connection updating his or her profile so the promotion is recorded. It is amazing how much information can be provided via this comprehensive networking tool.

On the other hand, some social media platforms are built more for social contact and activity. The best known of these is Facebook, although as described in various places in this book, the use of Facebook by businesses to secure greater engagement and collaboration with consumers is growing rapidly. On the social side, Facebook in one sense created the social media phenomenon by providing a simple tool for individuals to easily post information on current activities, comments on items of personal interest, and so on. It is said that there are some forty thousand Facebook posts every second. The activities on Facebook and other social media platforms have been given a massive boost in use and coverage with the advent of the smartphone and the tablet.

2. Follow the Lead

A second aspect of having fun is to be engaged with an ongoing activity of a family member or friend on social media. One very common activity in this regard is to follow somebody on his or her vacation at home or abroad. The ability to provide updates and photos can bring the vacation or adventure alive on a daily basis. The person can also provide commentary on his or her adventure, creating almost a real-time diary with the option for others to reciprocate with comments and reactions. People and places form the core of much social media activity. Of the top ten uses of Facebook, uploading photos is said to be number one.

The smartphone has also boosted the use of photos and video on social media, and there has been rapid growth in the use of photos and images in the social media experience generally. A survey from the Pew Research Centre[8] revealed that 54 percent of adult users in the US posted photo content on social media that they created themselves, up from 46 percent in the prior year. This shift has been helped by the growth of photo-based applications such as Instagram and Snapchat. As an example, this same report states that some 43 percent of those eighteen to twenty-nine years old say they use Instagram.

Of course, some of this can be a bit tedious. How many photos of "here I am in front of the Eiffel Tower" can we absorb and appreciate, or how

---

8 *Pew Research Centre, October 2013.*

many photos of my graduation do you really need to see? How far should you go down this path? As with many of the issues around social media, the answer is "it depends". Social media is very much about water finding its own level, and if you don't like what you're seeing, there is always the delete option.

I experienced a person on Facebook once who seemed to be endlessly posting material that I considered to be "non-value-added" and irrelevant to me. It was not offensive in any way but was simply over the top in terms of frequency. The "unfriend" option did the trick. Likewise, I followed a person on Twitter after a chance meeting at a conference. This person also bombarded the so-called Twittersphere with an amazing amount of material, so much so that I found it was simply adding no value to me at all. In the case, the "unfollow" option fixed the problem very promptly.

3. Share the Experience

The third bucket for me is the ability to celebrate with a wider community of friends and acquaintances, whether sharing birthday photos and experiences or simply highlighting a milestone in a busy week or month. It could also be the celebration of a particular achievement, such as a graduation from university. Celebration is a natural human desire and is particularly fun to share. Celebration is easy on social media, especially with the integration of smartphones and other social media applications. It is so easy to take a picture at a celebration, add a few comments, and have it posted on social media within a minute or so.

Special events such as weddings or birthdays seem to be particularly popular. A real-time upload of photos and comments can add a new dimension to these events and to their enjoyment by distant friends or relatives.

4. What You Can Learn is Amazing

For me, the major aspect of enjoyment from social media is what you can learn and the new threads of knowledge you can access. Perhaps a better way of expressing the point is to consider what you can't learn from social media. There is so much available from social media that many people wonder where to start. It is a bit like going into a restaurant with an extensive menu and wine list. Because there is so much choice, it is actually a challenge to decide.

The push of information from social media sites has exploded over the last couple of years. With the rapid growth of organizations having some presence on social media, people can access information from those organizations and participate in their activities in some way. This experience will vary from a very limited array of information at one end of the scale to full engagement and a two-way dialogue at the other end. In addition, organizations are increasingly using multiple forms of social media to connect with people globally, and they will use those channels to craft slightly different messages or levels of engagement.

In my experience, learning from social media is a highlight, and it gravitates around four broad categories.

(A) Here is the News

The first of these is the news of the day, and it is incredible to see so many media organizations falling over each other to reach out to social media sites in addition to their own direct channels. TV stations, for example, in addition to their normal programming will have strong presence on social media with updates or film clips or previews. Likewise, newspaper organizations will provide updates and stories on social media. It is particularly interesting to follow social media during a so-called breaking story and watch the flood of updates and comments from media organizations in real time. The news via social media is a feature many people now value because it provides regular updates on the big stories of the day, many of which are linked back to the main media site for more detail or background.

The emergence of consolidators of media information has allowed users to visit one site and selectively view information from many media organizations. The tablet application Flipboard mentioned earlier is a case in point. This tool provides in one place the major stories from many of the world's leading publications, and users can pick and choose which newspapers or journals they want to view. The service is free and provides a one-stop shop for this type of content.

A variation of the news of the day relates to news for emergency situations or warnings. This could be for road closures or accidents or warnings for approaching storms or other weather situations. These warnings and updates can be delivered promptly to a wide audience. Twitter is well suited to this kind of activity and is used widely by various traffic and transport authorities around the world as well emergency services.

(B) Professional and business information unleashed

Another learning dimension in social media involves professional and business activity. For me, this has been the real revelation in social media. Previously, if you wanted to get information or articles from a leading university, you had to either study at the university or subscribe to their journals, which were often expensive. On social media, significant material is now readily and frequently available.

For instance, material from the *Harvard Business Review* and similar publications is now accessible in ways that seemed just a dream even three or four years ago. *Harvard Business Review* material can be sourced in a number of ways, including a "follow" on Twitter or a "like" on Facebook. Many such publications are available via several social media sources.

This material can also be easily shared with friends or colleagues, and they in turn can reciprocate by sharing their material. In other words, this is not only about direct contact with the university or organization but about benefiting from all the material colleagues or friends may want to share.

The consolidators mentioned earlier also have entered this space. Consider Flipboard again. This tool also provides the one-stop shopping experience for some of these knowledge-based organizations, such as the World Economic Forum, *Harvard Business Review*, and so on. There are literally tens of thousands of sites from which professional or business information can be sourced, and a strong number of these are represented on social media.

(C) Special Topics and Interests

A third aspect of learning from social media is what I call "special topics", which could cover hobbies or sporting interests. Previous chapters discussed communities and how they can easily be formed on social media for a special topic. These special topics are too numerous to mention, but it is instructive to key in words on the search function on, say, Facebook. If you key in the word "golf" as an example, the golf-related pages will appear, and you can choose to like one or more of these. When you do so, those pages will generally post material to your timeline. The frequency depends, of course, on how often they choose to generate posts.

Imagine if you had interests in, say, golf, interior design, astronomy, and aviation. You could "like" several pages for each of these interests on

Facebook, for instance, and be presented with plenty of information from all of these sources each week and in some cases daily. Of course, this is from Facebook only, and you could do something similar on Twitter and other social media sites as well. The point is there is a huge amount to choose from, and the question is not how much is available but rather what is the right amount and quality for you.

(D) Advice Galore

Finally, there are facets of social media that can be described as being in the collective advisory business. There are numerous examples of these covering a wide range of interests and activities. For instance, TripAdvisor is well represented across social media and provides significant commentary about travel destinations. This is not all they do, but it is an important part of their offering. If you want to travel to, say, Hong Kong, you can go to TripAdvisor and look up various hotels, restaurants, and attractions in Hong Kong and view what other travellers have thought about their experiences there. These comments can also extend into conversations about the points of interest in Hong Kong in this case. This may not be a foolproof activity, but it nevertheless provides a strong avenue for comment and feedback that can form the basis for making purchasing decisions.

Mates and Buddies on the Journey

The idea of travelling companions has been around for centuries. People have always sought out mates to travel with for company or safety or simply to provide additional advice and counsel along the way. As the saying goes, two heads are better than one. The social media journey also generates a need for travelling companions. This is ironic in a way because by definition social media connects us to many people, possibly in many different parts of the world. Aren't these people our travelling companions? Well, maybe not.

In this context, I am referring to travelling companions as a few people close to us who can help with navigating our way through the do's and don'ts of social media. This could be family members or friends who have been involved in social media for some time. In a business context, this might be a consultant or subject matter expert who can offer specific advice relevant to the business. This is not a one-size-fits-all situation, but in my social media experience I have found the need for these mates along the way for two reasons.

In the first instance, it is good to have a sounding board, especially if you are new to social media. The mate or the buddy can play a key role in easing you into the understanding and use of social media and can also help you avoid some of the pitfalls. Much of social media is fairly intuitive and can be picked up easily. Indeed, social media is so popular partly because it is easy to use. But there are some aspects of social media that need to be understood right up front, and having a sounding board for this is important. One area where this is really important is in the setup. How you set up your profile on social media is crucial, especially the security and access settings. Most social media platforms have varying levels of access and security, and you need to understand how these work. Do you want your material or your participation to be more public or more confined? We have all heard people lament that they did not know their material was "going public". A simple check of the setup right at the start might have saved them the anguish.

Secondly, social media is changing so rapidly that it is almost impossible to keep up with all the new features and sites. In fact, the dynamics here are quite complex. We often think about all the changes in social media but sometimes forget that we are also changing. The way we use social media changes over time and what we want out of it will also change. Our expectations can also change depending on family or work circumstances. For example, if a son or daughter moves out of country for work, the parents will probably form a different view of social media even if they were previously nonbelievers.

The social media journey provides so much opportunity for enjoyment and for people to find new levels of connection, friendship, and knowledge. It is a means of providing new dimensions to social activity. But does it substitute for face-to-face meetings and social activity? The answer is no, but it does augment and enrich those experiences.

Personal friendship when I was young was heavily geared to people in the local neighbourhood or at school. Whilst these are still sources of friendship for our younger folk, they have now been significantly enhanced by social media, which enables people to be connected with a much wider community and one that is far more geographically dispersed than in earlier times. The really exciting part is that social media provides speed of connection and contact, but also the ability to share that with others.

Key questions to consider

- *What have been your memorable moments and experiences on social media?*
- *How much do you learn from social media and how can your experience be improved?*
- *Who have you used as your buddy (or buddies) on your social media journey?*

4

The Business Journey

Change is the law of life. And those who look only to the past or present are certain to miss the future.
—John F. Kennedy

Business and Technology Adoption

Technology has been a key enabler for many dimensions of social change, especially in the past fifty years. Think of the advances and social change emanating from computerization, the Internet, and the mobile phone, just to highlight three. For the success of these and other technologies, the business world has played a key role in their ultimate adoption and use. Indeed, business has driven the adoption of these technologies and has provided the critical mass and impetus for their commercial success.

For instance, the development and growth of computerization was largely driven by business demand for computing capacity to handle large data processing activities and later data analysis. As organizations grew in size and complexity and particularly in geographic spread, there was a strong demand for better ways of managing the large volumes of information that came with such growth. Large-scale computerization in the 1960s in particular filled this void and opened up many more opportunities for how organizations could expand and manage themselves effectively.

Likewise, the Internet and many of its applications were initially built with business, government, and university needs in mind, especially communications and information sharing. Corporate needs were also front and centre for shaping new approaches to communications technologies. I remember a senior US banker in Asia in the mid-1980s showing me how he used his organization's fledgling e-mail system whereby senior executives in various cities in Asia could send and receive messages overnight to and from their head office in the United States. It was somewhat clunky compared to the slick systems we have today, but it nevertheless put technology in the headlights in providing strong applications for business use.

As with the cases above, business led the way in adopting and using what the technology had to offer, and it was only much later that personal and home use became the norm. The advent of the PC in the early 1980s started the era of computerization being placed in the hands of individuals. With rapid developments in software, this social change gained rapid acceleration over the next ten years and beyond. Likewise, the development of the Internet meant that individuals could simply and cheaply access information, communications, and ultimately items of personal interest such as music, photographs, and day-to-day purchases.

But with social media, the pattern of adoption and use has been the reverse. The personal use of social media has led the way, and now it is business that is catching up, albeit very quickly. Social media from the beginning has largely been built with individual needs and use in mind, but there is no doubt that businesses and governments have rapidly expanded their social media presence. Check out the various social media channels used by your local retailer, your bank, or your local municipal authority. Many public sector agencies and organizations are also engaged in social media activity with citizens and stakeholders.

In chapter 2, I referenced a report showing the growing adoption of social media by the Fortune 500, especially highlighting the significant use of Twitter. Whilst this trend provides no conclusion or comment on the quality of the Fortune 500's social media activity, it does suggest a growing level of social media engagement for large corporations. Things have come a long way in just the last few years.

Social media now gives business, government, and organizations both large and small the tools and the opportunity for a different type of contact and interaction with their customers or stakeholders, and on a 24-7 basis. Technology has been a key enabler for social media. In particular, the advances of technology and especially mobile devices in the late 2000s have given social media the springboard for massive growth in a very short time frame.

Social Media a Key to Changing Business Models

But the issue for businesses, government, and other organizations is not just about gaining a presence on social media. There is a bigger picture here. One of the major shifts is that business models are under serious challenge from mobile technology, the Internet, and especially social media. This rapidly changing business model challenge is happening because the way that organizations relate to their customers, their employees, and their stakeholders is changing, and social media is driving and shaping much of this change. As a result, executives are on notice regarding the need for an urgent change of focus in organization capabilities and how these can help deliver greater business value.

Highlighting this point, Wal-Mart marketing chief Stephen Quinn is quoted as saying, "We have ROI [for social media] that's really strong—and it's transforming our organization. This level of engagement we now have with customers is changing a whole bunch of other aspects of our marketing".

Social media is playing a key part in this journey of business model change. In one of my blogs,[9] I outlined four organization capabilities that are profoundly challenged, and social media is integral to each of these. These are now re-presented and expanded further.

1. Moving From Customer Management to Customer Responsiveness

Historically, customer management focused on the relationship of a business to its customers and vice versa. Today, however, this relationship has changed dramatically thanks particularly to the explosion of social media in the past five years. The customer-to-customer influence (or C-to-C as it is known) has now escalated in prominence, and response to this development is now top of mind for most organizations.

As referenced in chapter 2, consumers today rely more on the comments and recommendations of their friends and family than on the promises from makers and sellers of products and services. Social media has

---

9 *"The End of Organization as We Know It?" An English View (blog), www.englishviewblog. wordpress.com, August 2012.*

provided a platform for such a dialogue and is shaping a new way that businesses interact and relate to their customers. Remember the key features of social media that were mentioned right at the beginning of this book—instant, transparent, and global. These features are having a dramatic impact on how businesses relate to customer contact, queries, and relationships. Hence, the need for responsiveness in this real-time customer environment is now a major challenge for business.

Customers have always spoken to each other about the products or services of an organization. In the past, this has tended to be somewhat sporadic and infrequent, but in the world of social media it has been revolutionized. Contact amongst customers on social media sites can occur quickly and easily, and as said earlier, this can occur across the globe as well. This C-to-C activity is one of the most powerful aspects of social media. It has major implications for how businesses reshape their business models to provide the required responsiveness to customer needs.

I was dealing with an airline executive recently after completing a series of strategic planning workshops. The executive was contrasting the challenges of managing customers today compared to ten years earlier, especially regarding customer loyalty. The executive summarized it this way: "Ten years ago the issue was how to collect more data on customers and their behaviour and considering what they might want. Today the challenge is how to respond to the real-time picture of customer needs and wants that is captured especially through social media".

Changes are emerging rapidly. Various consumer-facing organizations such as banks and retailers are transforming the speed and nature of their customer interactions and responsiveness. They are investing in capabilities to deliver a different level of engagement and outreach to their customers and the broader stakeholder community.

2. Shifting From Hierarchical Organization to Horizontal Organization

The hierarchical organization has been a stalwart over many decades with success heavily dependent on formal structure and segregation between the organization and its stakeholders. But technology is now dismantling such constraints as a result of the quantity and transparency of information that is readily and quickly available. This demands a flatter or more horizontal view across the organization and its stakeholders. The influence of social media across many consumer-facing industries is the rapidly evolving driver in this regard.

Organizations today face the reality that consumers or stakeholders seek rapid response to their queries or issues. The traditional way of dealing with customer issues was dependent on getting them to the right "department" and then having the right people investigate and report back. In many cases, this could be a long and cumbersome process that followed the typical vertical organization structure.

But with social media, customer issues are "live" and public as soon as they are posted, and rapid response is needed. An airline flight delay or lost baggage can quickly escalate into a major issue unless it is promptly addressed. Likewise a retailer faced with stock outs of popular products can publicly unleash irate customers very quickly. The traditional vertical structure to deal with customer issues simply does not work. A quicker and leaner way of responding is needed, hence the concept of the horizontal or flat organization.

Managing rapid response in the context of social media is a recently emerged capability for organizations across the board, whether it involves a complaint regarding service in a bank or an environmental issue with a mining organization. Executives are often nervous about rapid responses, especially in the context of corporate risk. What if an organization makes an incorrect statement in the heat of the moment that may go viral and cause further damage to the brand or reputation of the business? Each issue and the required response need to be considered on a case-by-case basis. What is true, though, is that consumers in particular seek quick responses and answers. Social media has given us a world of rapid-fire information and dialogue, and business models need to change accordingly.

3. Realigning From Product and Service Development to Collaboration

Various industries have begun to embrace the way they shape and deliver changes to their products and services. Traditionally, the development of products and services relied on surveys and various other tools for obtaining customer feedback and suggestions. Many of these tools are still valid and will continue to be so into the future. Once a product concept is finalized and released, a similar feedback process is used to test its success and define the need for any updates or modifications.

What has changed is the opportunity provided by social media to shape real-time development and the testing of new ideas, exchanging views on new concepts, and then using this environment to drive ongoing collaboration. The big difference from the traditional process is that this can be done often and at any time and in particular very cheaply. In other words, the feedback loop can occur rapidly and frequently, thus cutting down dramatically the time taken to gain feedback on product changes or launches of new products or services.

Retailers and consumer products organizations, for example, are now engaging with consumers in various forms of collaboration to drive new product development. US-based Wal-Mart went one step further with the concept of "Get on the Shelf Contest". This allowed people to submit a video of a product concept, with the online community voting on that product. Social media activity, especially on Twitter, was extensive. The product with the most votes was sold online and featured in selected Wal-Mart stores. This initiative was not only about product development and collaboration, but also was aimed at gaining stronger customer engagement via online and social media activity.

4. Moving From too Much Data to Much Greater Decision Support

Advances in technology have caused massive amounts of data to be created on a scale never thought possible just a few years ago. But recent growth in the field of analytics has meant that sensible conclusions and decisions can now be effectively made from these large volumes of data. This is especially true for the analysis of information emerging from unstructured data from social media. Think about the big changes happening for, say, banks and insurance organizations in areas such as customer segmentation and campaign management, pricing, and customer targeting. Much of this activity is enabled by smart analytics applied to social media commentary.

The issue is not whether these capabilities need to change but rather how quickly they will change organizations as we know them. The winners will be those organizations and industries that strongly embrace these capabilities as truly new change initiatives and deliver them accordingly to add value.

For many organizations, this will represent a major challenge. It does require the discipline to take a reality check on future directions and priorities. For instance, a transport business would need to ask about its capability in managing, say, an irate customer on social media. As part of this consideration, it would also need to assess how quickly such a capability can be developed or acquired, and the cost of the investment.

As French author and Nobel Prize winner André Gide once said, "One cannot discover new oceans without the courage to lose sight of the shore".

Social Media Means Real Business

Social media provides a significant opportunity for organizations on many levels and can help in various areas, including product and service development, customer queries, complaint capture and resolution, brand and image management, and so on. Whilst these terms have a private sector flavour, the use of social media in the public sector is just as important and can provide a significant benefit stream.

How organizations use social media is now often referred to as social business. In other words, how can organizations apply social media in all its forms to driving better business?

The type of business has a major impact on how social media is used and how it can deliver value. Figure 2 below shows the linkage between the types of business model and the intensity of social media use.

Figure 2 - Business Positioning For Social Media

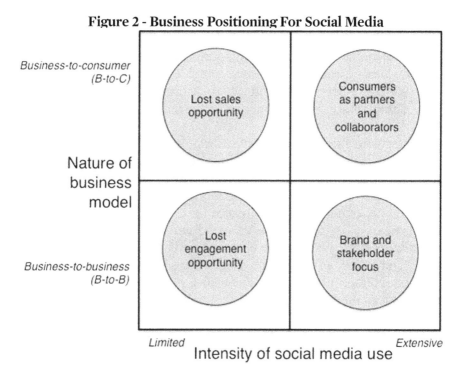

The vertical axis describes the extremities of the high-level business model. Some organizations are primarily engaged in doing business directly with consumers. These include retailers, airlines, retail banks, telcos, and so on, and this grouping is called business-to-consumer, or shortened as B-to-C. It is the same concept with government organizations except the term "citizen" can replace "consumer".

At the other end of the scale are those organizations that undertake business with other organizations and not directly with consumers. These could be organizations such as mining, industrial products, steel manufacturers, and so on. This is often called business-to-business, or B-to-B.

The horizontal axis shows the level of intensity of social media use ranging from limited at one end of the scale to extensive on the other.

Consider the lower part of the figure. In this B-to-B space, the social media focus is more about the overall brand and image of the organization. The target audience for messages here is not necessarily the end consumer as such or the direct buyers of the organization's products or services. In this situation, use of social media could be directed towards a broad range of stakeholders such as investors, the media, governments, and the community generally. Given the nature of a B-to-B organization, the messaging to these stakeholder groups could focus on promoting the following for the organization:

- Environmental policy and achievements
- Community activities
- Positive aspects of the end use of the organization's products
- Commentary on developments in the industry and global trends

The focus in the bottom right quadrant with its extensive use of social media is geared to delivering strong outcomes in the above areas. Organizations in this quadrant have a clear focus on the management of their brand and what they represent, directed across a wide range of stakeholders. Reputation is a strong motivator here.

Organizations in the bottom left quadrant would be those that have minimal or possibly no presence on social media. Many of these organizations will have strong stakeholder relationships by way of media presence and other channels of influence. But B-to-B organizations that have only a limited social media presence will potentially compromise the level and quality of their stakeholder engagement and underperform in this area.

On the other hand, the B-to-C area in the top part of figure 2 is quite different as these organizations deal directly with end consumers on a day-to-day basis. This typically involves not only direct contact between the organization and consumers but also includes the purchase of goods or services. The social media interaction is therefore much more intense and immediate. It is typically a direct and transactional relationship focused on the services provided or a particular consumer experience. In this case, the social media focus is more directed to engaging with consumers in connection with specific products or services and also to moving the consumer relationship towards one of greater trust and collaboration.

The top right quadrant of the matrix in figure 2 is directed at maximizing the impact of the interaction between the consumer and the organization by way of an intense level of social media interaction. This can take many forms, including direct conversations via chat rooms, product and service suggestions, and feedback. But this is not just about stakeholder management. This is about establishing and maintaining customer satisfaction and ultimately reaching a point of customer advocacy as mentioned in chapter 2.

This is the situation where consumers are advocates for a product or service and use social media to highlight their position. In other words, they don't just like the product or service but are prepared to endorse it publicly via social media. From the perspective of the organization, this is all about securing sales. Ultimately an organization dealing with consumers seeks to embrace those consumers as partners to help in developing and sustaining greater loyalty and in shaping better products and services.

At the other end of the scale, the top left quadrant of the matrix underscores the lost opportunity for sales with a lower level of intensity of social media interaction. Many organizations grapple with this point and struggle to find the link between the greater connections with their consumers via social media on the one hand and real sales on the other.

A recent paper[10] from Vision Critical outlines in some detail consumer research into the linkage between social media and sales. The study presents some compelling data and stories, and in particular draws out the idea of the three tribes of purchasers and how they use social media when they buy. The "Thinkers" use social when they are contemplating a purchase but before they research it in detail, the "Questers" research their purchase in detail via social media, and the "Leapers" are inspired by social media to actually make their purchase. The underlying theme is that there is a strong connection between social media and sales.

As a final point, I find it frustrating when some executives simply shrug their shoulders and say that social media does not apply to them. They are missing opportunities around the types of engagement outlined in the

10 *"From Social to Sale," Vision Critical, 2013.*

points above. This is especially true for those in this B-to-B category. The key point is that social media is relevant to all organizations, but there are differences in the way it is applied and the target audience to which it is directed.

Have the Right Business Conversation

Organizations have become more and more aware of the need to address social media in some way. It is a rarity today to find executives who have not considered the impact of social media on their organization and what options may be available to them. However, it is still a challenge to ensure the right conversation is conducted within the organization. Too frequently the social media conversation is directed to either the wrong level in the organization or to the wrong function. Let me illustrate.

Not so long ago, I was working with a business in the services arena that was growing rapidly. It had a dynamic leadership team strongly focused on gaining market share. In a conversation with the CEO, I asked about their social media strategy and how they viewed this as a strategic opportunity. The answer was that they thought social media was important and that they had asked the so-called young people in the business to develop the approach and how this could be implemented. On one level, it was admirable to have the so-called young people involved, and this gesture was appreciated within the business. Furthermore, it was also seen as a very contemporary statement by embracing the new joiners in the business, especially those fresh from university.

But on the other hand, this approach defied logic in so many ways. In fact, it sadly highlighted a virtual abdication of responsibility on the part of the leadership of the organization. Yes, the young people have a role, and their ideas and experiences would add much to the discussion, but the key point that I emphasized with the CEO was that the social media strategy and its approach are crucial business issues for the CEO and C-suite executives.

In another situation, I was speaking to a group of executives at a breakfast briefing and their view was also somewhat off the mark. They espoused the virtue of their decision to let their IT community come up with some options and really drive the social media agenda. The IT function of course has a key role in the development and the execution of the social media strategy, but it is only one factor in the mix.

The above conversations are not uncommon and, sadly, miss the mark. Moreover, they could be costing organizations lost opportunity in the marketplace or with their stakeholders. The conversation around social media is one that affects the entire organization and therefore must involve the C-suite. This is the case whether the business is B-to-B or B-to-C as outlined above, but it is particularly the case for a B-to-C organization. It also applies equally to government organizations, especially those dealing directly with citizens.

The business conversation needs to take into account a number of points. First, the social media activity will have an impact on all aspects of the organization in some way. For many organizations, this will be a very direct interaction with customers whereas for others it will be more around brand reputation and stakeholder management. But the point is that it is a business issue that needs to be considered as a whole and not just palmed off to one part of the organization to address.

In addition, the execution of a proper social media strategy will need the allocation of resources, and so the involvement of the C-suite is essential to ensure that the full business perspective is provided for these decisions. This is also important to ensure that the return on investment process is monitored and managed over time.

Finally, the social media strategy may need to change over time to respond to changes in the marketplace and to the actions of competitors. Earlier chapters have already highlighted the fast-moving nature of social media, which in turn underscores the importance of C-suite involvement in this journey and engagement in the changes that will inevitably occur.

Much More than Just a Website

Some organizations have taken a minimalist approach to their broader digital strategy. For instance, some take the establishment or refinement of their website as evidence of a clear digital strategy. Ten years ago the establishment of a website for a business was seen as being right out there. But today this is seen as providing table stakes only. This is but one small step along the journey and one that can be considered as foundational only. Of course, there are many types of websites out there ranging from those that provide information about the organization and its offerings to full transactional websites that offer full purchasing and delivery capability. Much of this is built around structured data and information flows.

Social media challenges organizations to lift to a whole new level. This is especially the case because social media is characterized by unstructured data and information. It changes the playing field in regards to what information is out there about organizations, their people, and their services and products. This is particularly so for those organizations that deal directly with consumers. For example, a traditional consumer survey would typically be issued to a range or sample of customers with structured questions and various responses set out possibly in multiple-choice format. Such surveys are popular and indeed still essential. Social media creates a new level in that it generates huge amounts of unstructured commentary and dialogue. It is about people talking and saying what they think. Therefore, new analytics tools and capabilities are needed more than ever to help to dissect and interpret the key messages and trends emerging from that data. What does it all mean and what business decisions can be made faster or more effectively based on analysing this data?

For organizations both large and small, the social media approach needs a commitment beyond merely a token presence. Businesses need to map out a strategy around their social media approach and execute well against it. Surfers know that catching a good wave requires keen judgment around positioning, timing, and agility. Each of these needs good execution for success, and this is particularly the case with social media. What track will your business embrace around social media and how will you shape that decision? Will it be a deliberate decision process or will it happen by default? How will you craft your positioning, timing, and agility?

Organizations need to consider and be very clear on where they want to be positioned with reference to the matrix in figure 2 discussed earlier in this chapter. This may need some thought if the organization is a mixed business or conglomerate. For example, a bank that is involved heavily in consumer banking and corporate lending will need to consider an approach that is tailored to each of the two parts of the business. In this instance, a one-size-fits-all approach will not work.

The development of a business strategy around social media will need to take into account a number of factors. The first of these and probably the most fundamental is the degree of connection appropriate to the organization. This is a fundamental but basic element for business and social media. For instance, the use of the "like" button on a Facebook page provides such a level of connection between consumers and an organization. It provides a channel for some basic connection with consumers and stakeholders, albeit a somewhat passive one. It could be that after a "like" very little feedback happens that is visible to the consumer. The question is how much is that "like" really worth to the business and is it helping the push for more sales and business growth? Many organizations are positioned in this somewhat basic level of social media activity. Whilst it could also be considered an entry point for businesses into the world of social media, it is relatively passive and largely a one-way process.

A second and more advanced element involves engagement, which is far more proactive and dynamic. This consists more of a two-way dialogue and flow of commentary and feedback. This approach invites and expects the two-way dialogue, but it means there is far more investment needed in the management of the process. For example, who is the person(s) in the organization providing the responses to the comments from consumers? How is this dialogue managed and what governance needs to be established to minimize risk yet deal with the issues raised? When confronted with this scenario, many executives feel very nervous regarding the possible exposure of their organization and the prospect of something going wrong in the two-way dialogue. Nevertheless, many organizations are pushing down this path as evidenced by the data presented earlier in this chapter regarding the Fortune 500 participation in social media. Businesses involved in the travel and hospitality industries are well versed in this area, and there are many examples of airlines, hotels groups, and restaurants that have developed a regular and well-structured dialogue with their potential and current customers.

The most advanced element to consider in the strategy is collaboration, whereby the organization uses social media to not only connect and engage with its stakeholders and customers but also to effectively collaborate with them in areas such as product and service development. This requires a level of maturity in the use and appreciation of social media and is not for the fainthearted. It challenges organization capabilities in the way it is managed, how it is communicated, and how it can deliver real value.

Remember also that this is not just simple commentary and thoughts passing between consumers and the organization. In most cases, it involves a transparent dialogue visible to participants across the value chain. This is still an emerging area and is in various stages of experimentation in different industries. As described earlier, for instance, some retailers have started to use social media to expand their product development footprint and the social media input to enhance their options and opportunities for new ideas.

In practice, the above steps would require some form of progression from connection to engagement to collaboration. It would be almost impossible to fast track to the collaboration activity without the real learning and capability building that comes from engagement. This field of endeavour is moving fast, and many more organizations are now undertaking these activities with some degree of overlap.

Managing the Nonbelievers

Social media has its advocates in many organizations and at all levels. However, there are many executives who sit in the nonbeliever camp and find reasons why social media in their organization would not work rather than developing a position on how it might add value to the business. Other executives may claim they support social media but do not participate in it personally and consider only a minimalist approach in their organizations. Social media can be the target of indifference for some executives, given some of its perceived unknowns and risks, and some resistance to change. Affecting a major change can be painful and difficult no matter how strong the business case or the need for change, and social media is viewed by some as being in the "too hard" basket.

So what can be done to positively influence the nonbelievers?

Plenty of material has been developed and written about resistance to change and how organizations can work with many different stakeholders to effect the required change. Various interventions have been developed to help organizations introduce change. For example, major new systems implementations are often supported by various change management interventions ranging from communications programmes and information sessions to significant training and personnel development activities. In one sense, all of these activities need to be used in the introduction of social media initiatives. After all, they represent changes in the business, and therefore common approaches to managing change should work.

However, there are some specific points with social media that need to be highlighted. In the first instance, social media initiatives need to be framed as business changes and not technology initiatives. This is not to demote the importance of the technology, but it must be the business changes driving the use of the technology and not the other way around. The so-called nonbelievers must have a clear view of the importance of the business change and how social media will help. For instance, a planned business change could be to use customer feedback to develop a new product format and to use social media as a major tool to do so. This is no guarantee that the nonbelievers will suddenly swing their support into gear, but it at least puts the discussion on a business footing rather than simply as a view about a piece of technology.

In addition, everyone at the C-suite level should have some personal engagement on social media so they understand how it works and can appreciate some of the dialogue. Unfortunately, I have seen organizations put a blanket ban on such activity, so that C-suite executives are precluded from hands-on learning and experience of social media. But it is still possible for C-suite executives to use mentors and others to show them what is happening in social media on a regular basis. The catch here is that it needs to happen regularly. There is no point in seeing what is happening on social media on a monthly basis. A month can be a "lifetime" in a social media context. It is essential to have almost a daily view to demonstrate how conversations evolve and change in content even in the same day. For executives in consumer-facing businesses, this is particularly important as the landscape changes so quickly. In my own case, it was not until I watched social media up close and personal that I began to appreciate how it worked, but more importantly, I also realized what it might mean for business and how value could be driven from a business perspective.

No matter the policy of the organization towards personal participation by executives, it is important to have some form of social media "mentor" for the C-suite who can provide guidance and feedback on an informal basis. This would typically be a person independent of the C-suite, but who is knowledgeable about social media and who can provide ready advice when needed. For example, it could involve a short meeting to discuss the latest forms of social media tools and how they are used. What are some of the latest trends on Pinterest, for example? What are the changes in the demographics of, say, users of Facebook? What are competitors doing? Typically this mentor comes from an external group or someone internally who has a passion and personal commitment to the use of social media.

The fourth and final point relates to having clear results. Nothing convinces a doubter better than a real-life example of success. Once I worked with an executive who was highly sceptical about using social media to attract young people into the organization's graduate recruitment programme. He reluctantly allowed some activity on Facebook and was somewhat chuffed later to learn that a number of good quality new graduates had become interested in the organization as a result of its Facebook page. This did not necessarily convert him completely, but it did start to chip away at resistance once some real results were demonstrated. Of course, he did talk about this example with colleagues and others, and that in turn helped to further reduce barriers to change.

Organizations have grappled with social media over time and there have been many false starts. There is no doubt that some organizations still regard social media with a healthy degree of scepticism and doubt. In some cases, there is a bias to inaction rather than the reverse. But overall, organizations are moving to embrace social media in a positive way, and this is part of the social change discussed earlier. There are important issues for organizations to carefully consider, such as brand reputation and customer engagement and advocacy. Organizations that are successful in this space think about social media from the perspective of what they really want to achieve from social media and the value they expect to be delivered. Whilst some of this is still work in progress, it nevertheless provides a real and evolving opportunity for organizations generally.

Key questions to consider

- *What plan does your organization have for engagement in social media?*
- *What type of business conversation do you propose to have with your executive team regarding social media strategy?*
- *Who are the nonbelievers in your organization and how do you plan to bring them on board?*

5

Challenges along the way

Patience is bitter, but its fruit is sweet.
                    —Jean-Jacques Rousseau

Keeping up with Rapid Change

Keeping up with the times has been one of those mantras handed down through the generations. I feel sure that family discussions over many generations have embraced this notion, although it may have been expressed differently in earlier times. The notion of keeping up with the latest things is a great motivator, and marketing gurus have shown how this can be exploited for strong commercial success.

Social media is no exception. New forms of social media are developed and deployed, and existing social media sites change their format or the way they work. New forms of social media now appear more frequently, and the landscape is changing rapidly. It was not always like this. Not so many years ago, Facebook achieved early dominance and virtually owned the social media space, but over time more players appeared and provided different forms of social media. The appearance of Twitter in 2008 took the world by storm, and Twitter now occupies a very prominent position in social media. More recently Pinterest has also grown extremely rapidly and is carving a significant niche in social media. Business websites will often have buttons to follow or connect with them via five or six different social media platforms. For instance, the retailer Tesco in the UK has connection buttons for Facebook, Twitter, Pinterest, YouTube, and Google+.

In addition, the existing players are constantly upgrading their features and providing more comprehensive experiences for their users. LinkedIn, for example, has in recent times introduced an influencer programme whereby LinkedIn members can follow thoughts, comments, and articles from high-profile individuals such as entrepreneur Richard Branson and British Prime Minister David Cameron.

How do we keep up with all this? How can we maintain our sanity in the face of all this change? I offer three suggestions.

1. Try it and Be Engaged

Firstly, try out the new stuff and give it a go. As with all things in social media, it is important to participate, and you will not know what a new social media site is like until you try it out. You can also check with friends or acquaintances about their experiences. One the great features of social media is that you can use it to test ideas or thoughts amongst your community. A simple question such as "I have just come across a social media site called [XXXX]—does anybody have experience with it?" can often help to answer questions quickly and by people you know.

I find that I need a solid month or two to really get used to new social media sites and to discover their strengths and weaknesses. I also find it takes a few mistakes (hopefully simple ones) to really understand how they work. Most social media sites have help buttons or help menus that can provide quick answers to most questions, and this can be a fast way to resolve queries or issues regarding use and functions. Chat rooms also offer an excellent way to resolve questions. If I have a query on how to use an aspect of social media, I always find there were many before me with the same or similar query. In fact, on more than one occasion I have found the chat rooms have given me quicker resolution to my queries than the social media help menu.

The same principles apply to upgrades or new features to existing social media platforms. New features are rolled out on a regular basis, and most of the social media sites will provide high levels of awareness and publicity around these changes. Nevertheless, it is important to embrace these changes as quickly as possible to take full advantage of the new functions.

2. Find Your Own Level

A second theme is to ensure that you find what suits your needs and level of capability regarding the new sites or the ones that have been upgraded or modified. The point here is that you may not like the new sites and want to drop them after some weeks of trial and error. There is nothing wrong with that, and indeed it is important to move on quickly if a site is not working for you. We are all creatures of habit, and if a new site does not work for us, then naturally we tend to revert to the activity in our comfort zone. In my case, I have tried many social media sites but have tended to gravitate back to the big three—Facebook, Twitter, and LinkedIn. I cannot give a full account of why this is so other than to say these are the sites that give me what I want on a regular basis and across both information provision and social contact. For others, their experience and position in this aspect will be quite different.

The other factor with familiar sites is the network of friends or contacts or connections we have. It takes time to build a group of friends on Facebook or connections on LinkedIn or followers on Twitter, and the longer we are engaged with those communities the harder it becomes to make way for other social media tools. In other words, the switching cost comes into play, and although it may not be a dollar cost per se, it nevertheless forms a natural barrier to change. Some people seem to manage multiple sites with great intensity on a daily basis, but I must say that I am not one of them. In my view, there is a limit to how much social media one can really absorb without simply acting as a pass-through channel.

3. Your Use of Social Media will Change

The third piece of advice here is to recognize that how you use social media will change. This is quite normal and is one of the dynamic aspects of working with social media. Individuals can change their use of social media even over a few short weeks or months. They may have engaged with a different group of friends on Facebook, creating a completely different dialogue. Alternatively, they may have several friends travelling abroad and the conversation and the times and frequency of contact may change significantly to accommodate these circumstances. The use of LinkedIn for some may change dramatically depending on current circumstances. For instance, if someone is seeking a new role or a personal reference from past colleagues, this may change the connections they have and the way those connections are used.

The business use of social media will also change for a number of reasons. These include the way that customers and stakeholders respond to the social media initiatives, how competitors respond, and, most importantly, how the organization perceives the value being delivered from its social media initiatives.

The test here is what works in your circumstances, and this means that as social media changes, individuals and organizations will also change in how they use it, which tools may become more or less prominent, or where time on social media is spent. Don't fall for the trap of simply trying to be trendy for the sake of it. By all means try out new social media sites and engage in their activities, but at the end of the day it is what works for you that is important.

The Personal Journey Can Have Challenges

Social media can provide a few interesting twists and turns, and sometimes the personal journey just does not work as planned. Because it is a highly dynamic environment that changes at an ever-increasing rate, it is inevitable that some things will not work out as hoped.

In the early stage of social media activity, too many people become very tentative and sensitive to early frustrations. Indeed, there can be a negative reaction based on a one-off experience or a single incident early in one's social media journey. For example, a slow upload of photos can be very frustrating for a first-time user and can lead to a negative perception of the social media site. The key here is to go back to first principles and consider the whole venture into social media as a journey and to accept the fact that there will be some frustrations and disappointments along the way. Staying with the journey especially in the early days is crucial.

An area where people can find frustration is lack of success in making connections or friends via the various social media tools. This is especially the case in the early days of social media activity. At one level, this may seem a trivial issue. After all, we know those with whom we want to connect, so let's just make it happen. But one of two things can happen.

Firstly, some invitations we send for friends or colleagues to connect with us may simply be ignored. Our first reaction to this situation is normally one of denial. Perhaps they have not received the invitation. Then there is the frustration or anger about why people we know would not accept our invitation. One of the salutary lessons I learned early in my journey was the fact that people are all at different stages of their learning curve regarding social media. Some may be real novices and may be lacking in confidence regarding what seems like a simple invitation. They may also be very infrequent users of the social media tools and therefore may take some time to accept.

One time I sent an invitation to someone to be a friend on Facebook. Nothing happened. Over the coming weeks and months I almost forgot I sent the invitation, but then some months later came the acceptance, much to my surprise. Later when I caught up with the person face-to-face, he felt no guilt at all regarding the delay to my invitation as his practice was to visit social media sites every few months and only accept new invitations at that time.

A second but related area concerns invitations that come from people we don't know at all or don't know very well. Some people have a firm rule that they will not accept invitations unless they know the person specifically, even if the person came highly recommended by a friend or colleague. Others will be more flexible depending on the type of social media. For example, following a stranger on Twitter is almost the norm whereas there is typically more of a personal filter applied to invitations to connect on Facebook or LinkedIn.

Challenges on the Business Journey

For businesses using social media, the challenges are somewhat different, and they relate much more to how social media affects the brand or the reputation of the organization. In particular, there is a question about how well the social media journey meets the desired outcome of the organization's strategy, a topic that was covered in more detail in the previous chapter.

One of the biggest challenges for organizations is managing any negative commentary on social media either from customers directly or the broader stakeholder community. Organizations are rightly fearful of any negative or sensational comment going viral and out of control. Comments that fit this category can originate with a disgruntled customer or someone who bears a grudge against the organization for some other reason. Whatever the reason, the issue at hand is how to manage a potentially damaging situation. On one level, this is no different from managing customer complaints and dealing with them quickly and in good faith. But on another level, the social media environment creates a whole new ball game because the complaints or comments are out in the open and visible to many people. This can quickly become a many-to-many dialogue, and a brand can be trashed and reputations damaged in a very short space of time. There is no simple solution to this challenge other than to point out that in most cases two things are crucial.

One is that the organization needs to respond with lightning speed to address negative comments on social media. This does not mean a response within a few hours or a day. It means an immediate response so that the organization is actively engaged in managing and influencing the damaging conversation that is occurring on social media. If this does not happen, the issue can balloon out of control, a legitimate fear of many organizations engaging with social media.

A second factor is the need to reinforce the key features of the brand that will help to mitigate any damage incurred. For instance, if customer service was the target of an aggressive conversation on social media, then once the immediate issue is addressed, the organization should highlight some the good things it is doing in the customer service space and perhaps some of the innovations it has introduced. Depending on the issue, this may need reinforcement over time.

Another factor in the business context is dealing with some of the noise or trivia on social media. In the earlier example where a retailer asked for suggestions for an ideal shopping aisle, many of the comments made were a complete distraction from the main game. One hopeful person even suggested the ideal shopping aisle would be one where all the products were free. It is good to see that optimism is alive and well. But in reality, much of this sentiment is simply noise in the system, and there will always be an element of this. Remember that social media provides a vehicle for open and unstructured comments, and people will make a wide range of remarks and suggestions. The challenge for organizations is to be able to filter the noise and the distractions from the good ideas that can and should be explored further.

Dealing with Some Nasties

I received a message one day on one of the social media sites saying, "Have a look at what they are saying about you on [URL address]". I had never seen a message like this and was highly suspicious, and I did not click on the URL, although it was tempting. This did turn out to be spam, and many people I know received the same message. In fact, one incident similar to this turned out to be a security breach.

As when dealing with any dubious contact, whether it be via e-mail or from a website, the name of the game here is caution. I have always found the following guidelines to be most helpful:

- Report it where you can.
- Ignore it on your system and don't click on any links.
- Move on.
- Reset password if needed.

There is not much more you can actually do. I have also found that any breach of security into a social media site often affects many users—in some cases, tens of thousands of people or more. In other words, you are not alone and you are not being targeted individually.

There is much written about unacceptable behaviour on social media and particularly that which can lead to bullying or criminal activity or exploitation. Authorities and regulators are rightly focused on stamping out such behaviour, and it is not my intention to further expand on this here. But there is an overarching point to underscore here, and that is to communicate with people on social media as if you are talking with them face-to-face. This can be easier said than done, and, sadly, unnecessary and combative exchanges do occur across social media. Remember, once you say something on social media, it is nearly impossible to expunge it.

Keep Social Media in Balance

Social media needs managing at the personal level in the same way that we need to manage our journey through life. It is never a smooth experience, and we must be prepared for some bumps along the way.

One of the challenges for some users is that social media comes to dominate their lives and reaches the point where interaction and acknowledgment are craved—in some cases to the point of obsession. Opportunities for obsession have always been there, whether playing sport or watching TV or engaging in an engrossing hobby of some form. One difference with social media today and its potential obsession is that it is so easily accessed from any device and is available 24-7.

It is easy to see how addictive social media use can become. I have found at various times that it can take up many hours of time and focus. For example, when travelling for business, social media can easily absorb time that would otherwise be idle. How many people are absorbed in social media activity waiting for planes at airports, for example? The people in an airport lounge or a bus or train carriage can look almost comatose with so many heads buried in devices checking the status of social media or e-mail.

I suggest you revert to two principles when confronted with some of these social media challenges. The first is to go back to first principles and recap what you want from social media and understand how the challenge fits into that context. Is the challenge merely an irritant or minor issue along the journey or is it something more fundamental? The second is to call in those two larger-than-life characters—patience and persistence. This is very important in the business context, as there can be so many twists and turns on the business journey.

Key questions to consider

- *What problems or challenges have you encountered in using social media and how have you addressed them?*
- *How do you approach new features or aspects of social media and manage the rapid changes?*
- *Is your social media activity balanced or is it dominating your life?*

6

Shaping Your Future Journey

Stay committed to your decisions, but stay flexible in your approach.
—Tony Robbins

Clarify What you want From Social Media

"Old habits die hard" is a familiar saying, and we see the inflexibility of old habits playing out in daily life in so many ways. Changing a golf swing or modifying the route taken to work is difficult because we become very content and possibly complacent with existing patterns or behaviours. Social media challenges some of our old habits in the way we interact with others and has a profound impact on how we as people and businesses relate with each other, with customers, and with employees. In the same way that the amazing Mars lander *Curiosity* opened up new horizons on that planet in 2012, social media is helping us define new horizons in the way we work, play, and live.

But does this just happen or do we need a more proactive approach to managing our involvement and engagement in social media? To gain the most from social media, a deliberate strategy is needed in how we approach and use it. We need to step back and understand where we are planning to go with social media and what we want to get out of it. Having said that, I will be the first to admit that in social media the adage "we don't know what we don't know" is alive and well. Even with a broad strategy in place, there is much experimentation and trial and error involved as well. This journey is not simply a straight line from A to B; there still needs to be some over-arching plan or roadmap to give us some semblance of direction.

The strategy from an individual perspective is not like a major corporate strategy where deep thought and analysis are conducted over many months, typically involving many iterations and meetings. Indeed, as individuals, we need to keep the social media strategy quite simple. What you are trying to achieve and how quickly you want to do so are two helpful thoughts to start the process. The answer may be as simple as being curious about politics or science on social media or perhaps wanting to stay better connected with family members who are travelling away from home, and these are very legitimate objectives. Or there may be a desire to build a higher profile or enhance your personal brand, a subject that is further discussed later in this chapter.

For businesses, on the other hand, the social media strategy requires much more rigour in the context of the overall strategy of business, and much of this is covered in chapter 4. The social media strategy will need to be framed around how social media can help the business to achieve clear business outcomes, such as customer access and loyalty, customer service and feedback, online sales, or employee engagement, to name a few. Each business will need to consider what new capabilities will be needed to manage a greater presence on social media. There is no point in creating a platform for customer feedback on social media if the business cannot respond and act in a timely way.

Many organizations have approached the world of social media by initially creating a Facebook page, for instance. But how that Facebook page fits into a strategic frame is the important question. What can businesses learn from the experience of being on Facebook? What comments are being posted about their products or services, and what level of interaction are they experiencing with customers? The learnings along the journey are as important as the journey itself.

Elements of your Social Media Strategy

A social media strategy needs to be embraced by individuals and especially by organizations. In developing this strategy, lessons can be learned from the game of golf, a global game of great popularity that is played by people of all ages and in many diverse locations. Various surveys suggest that some fifty to sixty million people across the world play golf regularly. It is a game of great challenge, but also one of enjoyment. It is also a game that is strongly dependent on individual performance, commitment, judgment, and adaptation to prevailing conditions.

Regarding social media, four lessons from golf are very relevant.

1. Have a Game Plan

Golfers know that a game plan is important. Each game is different depending on a range of factors including weather conditions and the state of the fairways. A good golfer will assess how to play the game in advance and whether more aggressive club selections are needed for the game because of prevailing conditions.

An individual seeking to embrace social media needs to have a broad game plan of what he or she is trying to achieve and how to go about it. This is not about the volume of thought but rather the clarity of thought. Be clear on where you want to head with social media, and, as stated earlier, it is important to create enough personal time and space to give it a go and get the most out of it. Is it more about using social media for business or professional activity or is its main focus going to be more on social aspects? Or is there a blend of the two?

At the same time, social media also needs some degree of experimentation or trial and error. Whilst such experimentation is valid, it is important to keep within the boundaries of an overall plan because otherwise the journey can become quite random and may achieve very little. A colleague of mine once showed me his command of an amazing array of social media tools, but there was a limited amount of time he could spend on any of them. In fact, he was doing justice to none of them and was spread far too thinly.

Business organizations will usually have some form of strategy or game plan, but how this strategy or game plan is articulated will vary widely. Social media is a key element of this strategy because it defines one aspect of how an organization connects with customers and stakeholders. As outlined in chapter 4, businesses need to have a clear view on how they want to use social media in the context of the business model they have.

2. Maintain a Strong Social Media Focus and Commitment

Golfers often lose focus or grow overconfident about their final score. They may have had a good first half of the game, but the score can turn badly on just one or two strokes or one bad hole. Top players have all too often seen the winner's trophy in sight, only to find it eluding them in the final few holes of the game.

Like these golfers, individuals should establish and maintain a strong commitment once they have embarked on their social media journey. In earlier chapters I spoke about the notion of giving it a go, but this must be done in a way to maximize the chance of success and enjoyment. A fleeting visit to social media sites from time to time will not provide a decent level of satisfaction or enjoyment and may cause disenchantment.

A friend once said to me that he had tried a social media tool for a couple of weeks and then lost interest. I suggest this person did not give anywhere near the commitment and focus that was needed to give it a go. As stated earlier, there is no simple formula here, but what is important is to dedicate sufficient time and effort to the task, especially in the early stages. In fact, it is essential to carve out some time for this on a regular and committed basis. It is a bit like fitness. A casual visit to the gym from time to time will not deliver the fitness benefits expected. It needs commitment to a regular and frequent programme.

Part of the strategy for organizations engaging in social media is to keep the focus on social media but at the same time allow for variations along the way as organizational needs change or as different social media tools or approaches become more relevant. Organizations can find social media challenging because it shifts communications and information flows to a totally different level. A business that has a very traditional way of connecting with it customers and stakeholders can be quite bemused with aspects of the social media experience. "What if there are comments about us that we don't agree with? How do we stop information going viral? What information are we giving up to our competitors?" These are some of the common questions that arise from businesses as they move into the social media space. Indeed, some of these questions can be so confrontational that some businesses never get past the very early steps in social media.

The key point is for organizations to embrace social media with the mind-set that if it does not work quite as expected, then make the appropriate changes. But it is important to stay with the journey. For instance, if customer comments are not as favourable as expected, perhaps some greater level of engagement is needed with those individual customers or the customer group as a whole. This is highly relevant information in the hands of the business that may not have otherwise come to light, and staying committed to the social media journey at this point is really important. There may also be a need to shift to different forms of social media or to change the way the interaction occurs, such as being more proactive by issuing information to customers on a more frequent basis.

3. Tactical Choices Really Matter

For a golfer, the tactics on each hole need to be carefully considered. The choice of club for a particular shot is most often cited as a key decision to be made. Likewise, the approach to the green is a tactical choice. Should the player loft over a nasty bunker or perhaps play a safer shot shy of the bunker but a little farther from the pin?

For individual social media activity, the choice of the right social media tools is of equal tactical importance. For an individual wanting to have more of a professional interaction with work colleagues and work interests, the use of LinkedIn would be a better choice than social media tools that are geared to more social commentary and the exchange of photos. It is important that the right tools are chosen to ensure individuals get what they seek from social media.

In the business context, the choices are of tactical importance on a number of levels. One is the choice of social media tools that will deliver the type of outcomes the business seeks. Is it Facebook or is it more of an engagement on Twitter or perhaps a mix of both? What other social media tools need to be considered? But a broader factor is the investment that the business needs to make in social media. What budgets and which people will be affected and how will all this be managed on a day-to-day basis?

Businesses will need to be very clear on their level of commitment and how resources will be allocated. A CEO once told me that his venture into social media almost failed because the business did not recognize that social media activities were much more than incidental or add-ons to the business. They need to be integral to the day-to-day business activity and funded accordingly.

4. Don't Complain About the Conditions—Deal with them

The final point involves the conditions in which individuals and businesses operate. Again, consider golf, a sport that is played in all conditions—the wind, the rain, the heat, and so on. The conditions cannot be changed, so golfers have to learn to deal with these variables and change their game or their gear accordingly.

Individuals using social media need to deal with whatever social media serves up to them on a daily basis. This is especially true in the early days of their social media activity. How friends respond to their various posts (or perhaps don't respond), how many friends or connections they have, and what kind of information they find are all factors and conditions that individuals will confront.

The surrounding conditions can also shift in the business context for social media. This is especially the case if any negative comments or some aspects of its activities as discussed above start to emerge about the business. Organizations need to deal with these factors and develop and execute the right mitigation strategies.

Organizations are likely to face at least three challenges in the social media conditions they experience. The obvious one is how engagement on social media occurs and what comments, both good and bad, are being made. Another major challenge is how competitors respond and how they engage with their stakeholders. This can be a threat but at the same time can provide a real learning experience. The third area of challenge is how social media itself is shifting both in terms of the demographics and the various tools available. New tools are appearing all the time, creating different audiences and interactions with business. For example, Instagram and Google+ have come on the scene in recent times and have established themselves quickly and with widespread acceptance and use amongst consumers.

Define Your Level of Participation

At its simplest level in either a personal or business context, social media strategy needs to address the fundamental question of participation and whether to adopt a stance in one of three forms:

- Passive participation
- Minimalist participation
- Full and active participation

These levels of participation need to be considered in a personal or business context, and the value for each will need to be assessed. The business considerations will involve more nuances and issues, but the principles are the same.

Passive participation is exactly what it says. It involves a presence on social media but with very limited or direct contribution of content. It could be someone on Twitter who only looks at Twitter traffic but who never makes any tweets. It could be people on Facebook enjoying their friends' news and photos but not contributing anything. Personally, I find there are many people with whom I am connected on LinkedIn who are silent most of the time and then suddenly appear almost out of nowhere with a "like" or "comment" on something I have shared.

For business, passive participation could involve a simple Facebook page providing a minimal amount of information and activity. It could be a gentle and low-risk entry into social media in order to establish a foundation from which to assess and develop further.

Is there anything wrong with this strategy? Absolutely not. This is a valid approach to social media, and from an individual perspective, if people feel they are getting value, this is perfectly valid. The argument could be made, of course, that they are not maximizing the value they could obtain, but that is another issue.

At the other end of the scale is the full and active participation strategy that involves the use of multiple social media channels on a frequent basis. This strategy is highly proactive and visible and involves engagement in many aspects of social media, including the regular contribution of material and sharing of information and comments. People who have adopted this strategy will typically have large networks of friends or followers.

For business, full and active participation involves engagement with customers and stakeholders and the development of real business opportunities and sales. As stated earlier, there is a need in this situation to embrace the right level of capabilities to enable the business to deliver and to gain value from its presence on social media.

Of course, in between these two extremes is the minimalist strategy, which may involve one or more social media channels but with a minimal level of activity.

Movement between these strategies is very common, and the whole area is quite dynamic. For instance, new users of social media almost always start at the passive end of the scale and move to minimalist and possibly to full participation quite quickly. Alternatively, some people may start at the passive end and remain there because that is what suits them and in their eyes gives them the value they want.

Your Personal Brand and Social Media

In recent times, much has been written about the notion of personal brand and how one's image in the eyes of others can have a profound impact in areas such as recruitment and career progress, personal influence, and self-esteem. Seeking out someone in demand is driven heavily by that person's personal brand and how others feel about that person. This is important in the workplace as people reach out for technical or job-related advice or for general mentoring activity.

On the social front, personal brand has a big influence on how friendship groups are formed and how different social activities unfold. A person who is not a team player, for instance, may gain a negative reputation as a result, and this will have major bearing on how people reach out to him or her. This individual's personal brand could be a real impediment to his or her work or social inclusion and activity.

Well, guess what? Participation in social media has now made this issue more visible and potentially more challenging. Social media can be an important part of the mix of factors that influences one's personal brand, but it does depend, of course, on the level of participation. Those who are passive participants will not have much impact on their personal brand compared to those with full participation whose personal brand will be highly visible. Figure 3 below shows a visual representation of the link between social media and personal brand.

Figure 3 - Social Media and Personal Brand

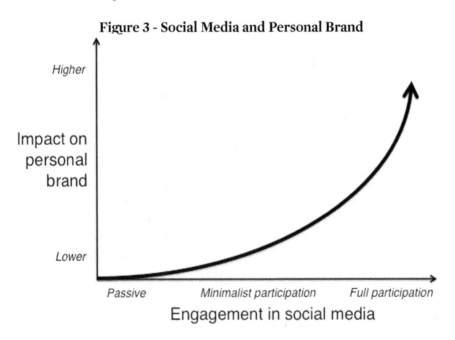

The horizontal axis highlights the level of engagement in social media, which was described more fully in the previous section of this chapter. The vertical axis highlights a higher or lower impact on personal brand. The figure illustrates that the more active you are on social media, the greater the impact on personal brand, whether positive or negative. Any participation can reveal things about you, but full participation on social media can reveal much about you as a person in terms of interests, beliefs, and attitudes. What you contribute by way of articles or opinions can also show your inclinations or tolerance to certain issues.

Let's face it: there is a lot of stuff floating around on social media that tempts us to respond wildly in support or vehemently in opposition. Your responses often define your thinking in the minds of others or reveal a bias or a political or social leaning. Your responses can also show the type of person you are and whether you are compassionate, highly driven, or ambitious. Some people like to use social media as a giant soapbox to air their views and to throw their opinions out there for comment and challenge. The important point is that you may not intend comments or opinions to be interpreted as they are. From the perspective of personal brand, it is all about how others see and interpret what you say as you participate in social media.

The transparency of social media means that participation feeds directly into your personal brand. What is said on social media becomes an integral part of your personal brand—both the good and the bad. Various filters and restrictions can be placed on who sees what on social media, but it is fair to say that anything said on social media will affect your personal brand in some way. No matter what filters or restrictions you use, some community is going to see what you are saying or the articles and content you are sharing.

To illustrate, assume you have one hundred friends or followers on whatever social media platform and that each of them has fifty followers. Let's also assume you send a comment that is visible to your one hundred friends. That means your comment has gone to one hundred people. But if each of them forwards or copies your comment to each of his or her fifty friends, it starts to get interesting.

In this case, the comment you sent to your one hundred friends has now gone to an additional five thousand people (one hundred of your friends times fifty of each of theirs). I have kept the math simple to illustrate the point, but this is how things go viral across social media and how theoretically a simple and innocent comment on your part can end up becoming a global storm very quickly. For most of us, this is not and will never be an issue. Nevertheless, there is an important principle involved here, namely that what you say on social media does affect your personal brand in some way.

Take recruitment, for example. A recent Jobvite survey[11] concluded that 92 percent of US companies were using social networks and media to find talent in 2012, up from 78 percent from five years earlier. Anything on social media is in play when it comes to the job market, and this has a direct link to the personal brand.

Many people will caution you about what you should and should not say on social media, and this is good advice. But the bigger picture is how the personal brand overall is affected. Does the résumé describe a person who seems to be quite rational and level-headed, but social media activity shows a person of strident opinion and volatility? Clearly in this case, the personal brand could be compromised.

In the end, personal brand is made up of many factors, including social media. How people participate in social media will have an impact on personal brand in some way, so it is important that involvement in social media is understood and managed with this in mind.

Applying Past Business Learnings to the Social Media Journey

Some of us can remember the early days of computerization. This new and exciting concept brought with it many questions and uncertainties for businesses and for individuals. There was a sense that computerization was inevitable, but it was mixed with much ambivalence about what its real impact might be. Indeed, there was scepticism about how far this new activity would go and the extent of its impact in the future. It was seen initially as a new thing for organizations to use, and the concept of transforming organizations as well as daily lives through computerization was not widely appreciated. Indeed, the term EDP (electronic data processing) was the rather passive term used as a descriptor for what computerization meant and how it was viewed.

Today we find ourselves at a similar point regarding social media and its potential impact on organizations. Whilst business today is moving with greater speed on this issue compared to the emerging era of computerization, there are nevertheless some interesting parallels in the journey.

---

11 *Jobvite social recruiting survey, July 2012.*

Firstly, the full extent of the transformation opportunity is still to be fully recognized. Many organizations are clearly experimenting with what social media can mean for them and their industry. But how many organizations are actively shaping and articulating social media strategies into their forward thinking to drive real transformation? A second parallel is the extent of understanding and involvement by the C-suite. Many executives are treading rather cautiously in social media and as a result may be missing opportunities to find new revenue streams or shape new opportunities with their customers. How many executives are really engaged in social media activity?

So what should organizations be doing regarding social media and lessons from the past? There are three things requiring senior management attention across many industries:

- The C-suite needs to be involved personally in social media to experience firsthand what it means. This will help to form a view on how social media can add value to their organization. In the early days of computerization, it was not until executives experienced its "touch and feel" that they were able to grasp its power and future significance for their organizations.

- There needs to be a real focus on social business strategy, which is elevated to the senior executive team for planning, discussion, and tracking. This is a senior executive responsibility as it represents a true transformation opportunity. It does not reside in just one function of the organization. The early days of computerization had responsibility sitting with the "EDP" department rather than across the broader executive team. Real transformation potential was unlocked only when the senior team became engaged more broadly.

- Finally, it is important to recognize the learning curve that will be confronted in social business. There are many do's and don'ts, but there is no simple formula or one-size-fits-all approach. Organizations need to apply all the dimensions of managing change to achieve success. The early days of computerization were characterized by the challenges of managing change and driving real value, and social media is no different today.

Your future strategy for social media is an important facet of the journey and gives you some definition about how to plan and respond to different challenges and opportunities on social media. Whilst this has obvious relevance to organizations, it is just as important for individuals to put some planning and thought into their social media journey. Some journeys can be totally random, and these can be a lot of fun. A trip done off a whim or on the spur of the moment can be very satisfying. But in the total scheme of things, most journeys benefit significantly from some degree of planning so the direction of the journey and its activities along the way provide maximum opportunity. Social media needs even more thought given it is relatively new and is changing so quickly.

Key questions to consider

- *What is your social media strategy?*
- *How will social media help to shape your personal brand?*
- *What will you do differently in social media starting now?*

7

Tips For the Journey Ahead

Wherever you go, go with all your heart.
                                        —Confucius

If i Only Had Time

A question I often hear is "How much time do you need to put into social media?" Whilst I understand the point, it is actually the wrong question to ask. A better question would be "How much effort do you need to invest to get what you want from social media?" This is particularly the case for businesses looking to gain a greater level of social media presence.

People who have a strong involvement in social media will say that social media for them is not an additional activity but rather an integral part of their daily routine. It is not just an activity but a part of life and in one sense is no different from having a regular meal or going to the gym or taking the dog for a walk. This is an important point as a lot of people will claim they are too busy or there is no time because they are travelling, and I hear these claims all too often.

The start of the social media journey is the hardest, especially when involvement in social media is seen as an additional activity that has to be accommodated somehow. Moreover, it is often seen as discretionary activity, which is a real challenge at the start of the social media journey.

There are two fundamental points about the amount of time needed. The first is there is no escaping the fact that an investment of time is needed. If you want to become good at a sport or a card game, you have to invest the time to learn about it, to practise it, and to experience it. I have seen people take a golf lesson, for example, and then fail to play a game of golf for another four weeks. Any retention from the golf lesson is probably minimal by that point so the opportunity has been wasted. A more productive approach would be to have some solid practice after the lesson to consolidate the learnings or at least to position the lesson much closer to the golf game.

The beginnings of the social media journey are a bit like this. Dedicated time is essential to experience and practise what is needed, especially to gain confidence and a degree of competence in the use of social media. But over time, as you become more familiar with the social media playing field, there will be a tipping point where the time invested in social media starts to become the norm.

It could be, for example, that you spend thirty minutes at the start of every day on social media over morning coffee. This may seem a bit intrusive, but it can be an important part of building the routine of participation. Others might spend time late in the evening. Another pattern for some is to spread the activity across the day as mobile devices facilitate social media activity at any time and in any place.

A second aspect to the question of the time required is that the amount of time itself does not really matter—to a point. There is no hard and fast rule on this. The value you get from social media should be the measure, and it is the one that matters most. It does not matter if you spend thirty or ninety minutes a day on social media, as it is far more about the quality of content that satisfies your needs. This will also depend heavily on the way you use social media and whether the major focus is on the social aspects or information aspects. Seeking information may occur for some on an as-required basis perhaps a couple of times a week or month, whereas those who focus on the social side may check in on a daily basis to see what is happening in their network. These are just two examples, but it is important to understand that everyone will have their own pattern of activity and that the times and frequency of social media activity will vary significantly.

There is also an extreme situation where some people are totally obsessed by social media and seem to be absorbed on an hourly basis. Suffice to say that the addictiveness of social media does need to be managed. Social media is a part of modern life but should not be seen as modern life itself. Constantly waiting for the next tweet or the next post from a friend on Facebook does not seem to me to be a great use of time in the total scheme of things.

Beware the Menu Effect

One aspect of social media that challenges many individuals and businesses alike is simply the amount of choice that is now available both in terms of the number of social media applications that can be used and how they can be applied in many different ways. It is interesting to reflect on Myspace, a social media service launched in 2003 that for several years was the most visited social networking site in the world. At that time, the social media choice was expanding rapidly, but by today's standards was still limited in size and variety.

Over time, Myspace was challenged in its dominance of social media. Facebook overtook Myspace in 2008 as measured by unique worldwide visits, and the social media growth since then is a matter of history. The phenomenal growth of Facebook has been well documented, but other social media applications have also exploded in growth. For instance, Twitter, Google+, Pinterest, and Instagram are showing extremely strong growth. According to socialtimes.com,[12] usage of Twitter grew 44 percent from June 2012 to March 2013, and Google+ grew 33 percent in the same period. How we make personal or business choices in this rapidly growing social media landscape is a challenge.

In addition to the daunting choice of social media, there is also the question of how social media has become part of the daily routine and not just an add-on. It is becoming more integrated into daily life and routines. This in turn affects the choices we make and how we use social media. Socialtimes. com indicates that almost one-quarter of Facebook users in the United States log on at least five times per day. This is an example of the choices that people make and the impact these have on their daily activity and routine.

But how do we choose amongst all the options and the ways that we can engage with social media? How do we manage the menu of choices and options to consider, and how do we do so in the context of the rapid change occurring all the time?

---

12 *"The Growth of Social Media: From Passing Trend to International Obsession," SocialTimes, January 2014.*

For most people and businesses, this menu effect means that the more choices that are available the more focused we have to be in understanding and defining what we want from social media. As described in earlier chapters, it means we have to be very clear on what we want to get from social media and therefore how we engage and use various aspects of social media. The variety is such that it forces us to choose and at least prioritize how we use it. There are some social media "junkies" who "multiprocess" across many forms of social media on a daily basis, but I suggest this is more the exception, and that for most people and organizations some sensible and measured choices are being made.

The choices around social media have a knock-on effect in that social media organizations themselves are scrambling to build more and more features and functions into their systems and to widen their appeal to users. This in turn is creating some convergence of features across various social media tools. The ability to use photos, for instance, has moved rapidly in this direction. One example of this is how Twitter has recently started to allow some use of photos in the content of Twitter feeds. The rapid rise of Instagram (now a part of Facebook), whose focus is on photos, is another example of choice in social media and changing customer behaviour. The value proposition to users of individual social media applications (whether for business or personal use) is changing rapidly and is a moving target.

When Do We Get There?

Many people have asked me where all this is heading and where it will end. The answer is both precise and vague at the same time. On the one hand, the social media revolution is about major social change in the way that people and businesses communicate, interact, and collaborate. We could rightly expect this change to continue and to expand in both breadth and scale. But on the other hand, we really don't know where it will take us ultimately and where we will be in, say, a generation. Mark Zuckerberg, the founder of Facebook, is quoted as saying, "I'd love to improve people's lives especially socially. Making the world more open is not an overnight thing—it's a ten-to-fifteen-year thing". Given the massive change that social media has brought over the last five years, the degree of change over the coming five or ten years and more becomes a tantalizing proposition.

Where we get to in social media and how long this takes will depend on many factors, especially whether we are considering the personal or organizational perspective. Overall there are several major considerations that influence where social media will take us and how fast.

The first of these is that social media is changing at an exponential rate. What is available as social media tools and applications is a rapidly growing space. In roughly ten years, the social media phenomenon was defined, and in that time, numerous social media tools emerged. The high-profile ones and their "birth years" include:

- LinkedIn 2003
- Facebook 2004
- Twitter 2008
- Instagram 2010
- Google+ 2011
- Pinterest 2012

If this has all happened in about ten years, what could possibly occur in the next ten years and beyond? I wish I had a definitive answer to this, but what we can say with some certainty is that the social media genie is well out of the bottle and that future change will continue to accelerate in this arena. Social media is both feeding on itself and redefining itself over time as new uses are found for it and as adoption rates continue to grow in all age groups and across countries and regions of the world.

Rapid changes are also occurring in how social media is used. Ten years ago, who could have pictured how major organizations and government agencies all over the world have moved to bring social media into their daily activities and interactions with customers and stakeholders? Whilst there is still a way to go in many industries and organizations, the change in the social media footprint in business in the past five years has been staggering. Who could have imagined how individuals can now engage with each other and with businesses in a range of activities such as product development and service improvement?

The scale of use is another dimension in the rapid change of social media. From a personal perspective, the number of registered users for Facebook (over one billion) or Twitter (half a billion) is phenomenal. Mark Zuckerberg from Facebook sees five billion Facebook users in the future almost as a personal mission. For business, socialtimes.com indicates that over 90 percent of marketers in the United States use social media for business. That is a broad categorization, but the point is that social media is moving front and centre in terms of business development and growth, and as social media business opportunities develop, this will expand even more.

A second consideration regarding the future journey is that social media is fundamentally about social change. This is a journey about social change the likes of which the world has never experienced before in terms of speed and scale. When social media first appeared on the scene, many saw it merely as a new way to connect with others in their network. It went beyond the formality of e-mail and provided another channel to reach others who were away from home or in other places far away. But over time, the notion that social media is about more fundamental social change has been recognized. Because it is a social change, it means it is hard to predict, it will not follow a linear pattern of development, and it will feed on itself. In other words, social media will influence social change and vice versa. As outlined in chapter 1, the core of social change in social media is the intersection of the three aspects of connection, community, and collaboration. The three of these together make for powerful social change over time in terms of the way that people behave and interact.

A final consideration is that digital access is changing and improving all the time, and this has major implications for the growth of social media. For individuals and businesses, one of the most profound technology changes has been the rise of mobile devices including smartphones and tablets. Much of this has occurred in the past five years and has redefined the landscape for social media and the way people connect with each other and with business and government.

According to a Cisco report,[13] by the end of 2014 the number of mobile-connected devices will exceed the number of people on earth, and by 2018 there will be nearly 1.4 mobile devices per capita. Their data suggests there will be over ten billion mobile-connected devices by 2018. This proliferation of devices means that access anytime, anywhere is here right now, providing enormous fuel to the growth and spread of social media.

Another aspect of digital access is the degree of readiness and capability across different economies. The Boston Consulting Group recently produced a paper[14] that showed an index of how different economies are placed in terms of their digital readiness. Their so-called e-friction index considered four factors, namely infrastructure, industry, individuals, and information, and compared the relative impediments to achieving each of these between different countries. Whilst this material is focused on the broader digital economy and comparisons between countries around the world, it nevertheless follows that a greater efficiency in the digital economy will also be a key enabler to the growth and use of social media. Many governments around the world now have the digital economy as a major policy issue on their agenda.

---

13 Cisco Visual Networking Index, Global Mobile Traffic Forecast Update, 2013–2018.
14 Greasing the Wheels of the Internet Economy, Boston Consulting Group, February 2014.

Take Control of Your Journey

Exhortations to take charge of one's destiny or activities are often heard in various aspects of life. In sport, for instance, terms such as "take the ball and run" or "lead from the front" are heard. In business and in personal life, such terms as "seize the day" and "take the initiative" are also familiar.

So it is with social media—one needs to take control of the journey and make it happen. Other than having a mate or a buddy as described in chapter 3, nobody is going to hold your hand in making social media happen for you. As stated earlier, things may not always go according to plan, but what is important is to take control of what happens and be proactive. Getting the most from social media needs a deliberate strategy and commitment as outlined particularly in chapter 6.

Let's be frank here. Social media can run rings around people if they let it and cause them either great frustration or, at worst, some real concern or anxiety. I have seen it in individuals and also in organizations where the social media exercise becomes a real threat rather than a positive personal or business opportunity. As I've said all along, the social media experience will vary dramatically from person to person or between organizations even in the same industry and location. But some common threads do apply across the board.

In the first instance, an individual or organization must drive proactively any presence on social media and its associated activity. There is one slight exception to this and that is for organizations responding to customer issues on social media. In such a situation, the nature and volume of social media traffic may be quite unpredictable, and therefore the level of proactivity may be reduced. But even in this case a solid social media strategy will ensure that the right level of resources and responses are shaped and delivered on social media in a timely way.

Secondly, it is important to monitor and measure in some way how the social media journey is going and what changes if any need to be made. Is the involvement in social media meeting its objectives and delivering the required outcomes or is it a distraction? Too many people—and organizations, for that matter—endure a poor experience with social media that is not delivering what it should and then make things worse by failing to modify their social media approach promptly. An example is an organization that is struggling to gain much real business via social media, but which is experiencing negative commentary on social media because of a product recall. In most cases, resolving the product recall issue on social media will need to be sorted with some urgency, and probably with a major change of emphasis at least in the near term. Then the focus can return to using social media to grow the business.

Finally, think of the social media journey as an exercise in creativity and not just a static experience. What different things can be tried either in reaching out to friends or as a business reaching out to customers? Just as in real-life travel, where journeys can be reshaped with different approaches and places to visit, the social media journey can also be recalibrated to include many different aspects of what social media has to offer.

In conclusion, my social media journey has been fascinating, and one in which I have encountered many twists and turns. My scepticism many years ago at the start of the journey has given way to enthusiasm and excitement over time. I have learned a lot along the way but have a lot more to learn, and that is the exciting nature of the social media journey and how it unfolds. We do not really know how social media will be shaped and positioned in five or ten years' time. But what I can say with some confidence is that it will continue to be dynamic, ever changing, and provide opportunities for greater connection, community, and collaboration amongst individuals and between individuals and organizations in both the private and public sector. To date, the journey has provided some challenges but also many rewards along the way. It has been most exciting to be a part of this journey and to experiment and try different things along the way. Long may the journey continue with its challenges, its opportunities, and its multitude of experiences.

Key questions to consider

- *How will you allocate time to social media?*
- *How will you consider choices that have to be made around social media and how to participate?*
- *How will you take control of your social media journey, and what challenges do you anticipate?*

About the author

Matt English is an independent business commentator, public speaker, and strategist based in Melbourne, Australia.

His business career has spanned some forty years, including senior roles as a partner with PricewaterhouseCoopers and IBM. He has lived, worked, and travelled extensively in Asia, Europe, North America, and Australia.

Over this time, his career has embraced three main areas:

- Strategy consulting focusing particularly on business model change
- Development and dissemination of thought leadership material for the C-suite
- Shaping and delivery of executive-level education

He has specialized in consulting with major clients in the areas of organization change, especially the re-shaping of business models.

Matt has been involved extensively in the development, publication, and presentation of innovative thought leadership covering various topics for senior executives across Asia Pacific. He has been directly involved in the development and deployment of five major global CEO studies and has travelled widely for their presentation and discussion.

Matt is active on social media. He sees it as a major vehicle for transforming personal connections, and one that is integral to the transformation of business and customer relationships. As a baby boomer, Matt has been fascinated by the enormous social change that social media is bringing to business and to society more broadly. He sees is as re-shaping the way people behave, how they interact with each other and how business is done.

He has a bachelor of commerce degree from the University of Queensland in Brisbane, Australia, and a master of business administration from IMD in Lausanne, Switzerland.

www.ingramcontent.com/pod-product-compliance
Lightning Source LLC
Chambersburg PA
CBHW061015050326

40689CB00012B/2655